Balance

It is yours if you want it

A Practical Handbook and Workbook

for Finding Balance

during Life's Difficult Moments

Suzie Doscher

For permission contact the author: www.suziedoscher.com

First Published in 2014 by CreateSpace Independent Publishing Platform

Cover design by JuLee Brand for Kevin Anderson & Associates

Cover image by Suzie Doscher

Second Edition – Revised and updated

ISBN: 978-1723095283

Dedication

I dedicate this book to all the "mistakes" I have made in my life that led me to the place where "something has got to give." I believe "mistakes," or lack of better judgment at the time, are in fact opportunities to learn from. I have made plenty and without all of them I would not have found the courage to make changes, grow into my skin, keep moving right along—becoming a better version of myself. As a result, I am happier than I have ever been within myself.

I am grateful to my parents for moving us to Switzerland at an early age. Growing up in a multicultural environment offered such wonderful and valuable life lessons. Their positive 'can-do' attitudes are admired to this day.

"Where there is a will, there is a way."

CONTENTS

INTRODUCTION

The moments when you feel vulnerable, unsure of yourself, or ineffective in a difficult situation are in fact opportunities.

Opportunities are the *beginning of change.*

This book is about *change, beginnings,* and finding *balance.*

Developing life skills to handle yourself more effectively in difficult moments brings about important changes in the quality of your life. The knowledge gained from self-help books, videos, lectures, podcasts, webinars, etc., while helpful, will not make a lasting difference unless you have these life skills to apply in daily life. This book will support you in developing new life skills. New life skills equal new behaviors. I like to think of life skills as tools – for "my toolbox for life."

What you will gain from this book is clear and uncluttered guidance in straightforward language with no gimmicks. I address the difficult and stressful moments in which you wish you had someone to talk to, to give you some encouragement, support, and strength. There is no balance where there is stress – stress contradicts calmness and happiness.

The Workbook section allows you to explore where you stand relating to issues from your past, where you are in the present, and where you wish to be in the future. I suggest a new journal for you to write as much or as little as you wish.

Everyone has their own definition of balance, just as each of us has our own definition of success and failure. It does not mean the same thing to everyone and the definition changes according to circumstances and age. Take a few minutes to think about what balance means to you and then dive in!

FIND BALANCE –
WOULD LOVE TO, BUT WHO
HAS THE TIME!

In my own life one of the important realizations was that balance is possible and it was mine if I wanted it. What followed was a fair amount of self-reflection, openness, and honesty with myself. Setting aside time to explore my definition of balance, by questioning what was missing and what I was already doing successfully, was time well spent.

Since then I have a good grasp on the various elements of day-to-day life. For me personally knowing my heart and mind are working together is what keeps me balanced. The sense of calm, of being grounded and clearheaded, motivates me to keep my life in balance.

Choosing to create balance will reflect in these six areas of your life:
1. Physical
2. Mental
3. Emotional
4. Social
5. Financial
6. Spiritual

Each one is important and will require consideration, attention, maintenance, or upgrading throughout your life. Not necessarily at the same time, or in equal amounts; nevertheless, all deserve attention. It would be impossible and unrealistic to believe that each can have a "full service" all of the time. So choose to focus on which area is being neglected the most at that time and see if it makes a difference. If you choose to socialize more but are not getting enough sleep, you might have chosen the wrong area to nurture. Choose your priorities carefully. All elements are interrelated; balance will be present when all six are respected.

Most of us spend a large part of the day at work. Making sure the remaining hours offer some form of nurturing, reenergizing, is vital. There is a difference for single people versus married, with or without children, whether you travel, live internationally and interculturally, etc. Choose the area most in need of attention and nurturing.

The groundwork of living in balance is knowing yourself. For this it helps to be connected to your core values. Think of them as the "bricks in your foundation." Reconnecting with your values and aligning your life with them is vital to finding balance.

Your values are what make you tick. They show you how to prioritize, what is important to you, what allows you to feel fulfilled. Examining my own core values, I realized how vital "open communication" and "nature" are to me. When both are present in my life I feel a sense of balance.

Six motivators to encourage you to achieve a more balanced life:
1. *Emotional Strength:* By gaining emotional strength, even on the bad days it is easier knowing what it will take to turn it around. This knowledge offers you a sense of grounding and balance. When you know yourself better you automatically know what has to be done.
2. *Decreased Stress*: Less stress offers time for more pleasure.
3. *Physical Energy:* Physical energy will return once you are prioritizing better, doing less, and nurturing your needs more successfully.
4. *Sleep:* Sleep – a better night's rest. With a more balanced lifestyle, sound sleep is easier to find. Your mind will not keep you awake as often.

5. *Compassion:* Compassion and empathy will come more easily. With a more balanced life you have more time to "feel" and "be" rather than only "think" and "do."

6. *Balance:* A balanced person is a better person. People will be drawn to you because being in your company makes them feel good. A person who feels good about themselves and their life creates a lovely energy to be around.

The benefits of creating balance reach beyond you and your life; the people around you are positively impacted as well. How does it sound to feel happier, wake up with energy, and plan your day realistically to achieve what you set out to do? There might be obstacles along the way, but when you are balanced your coping mechanisms kick in, you deal with the issue and get on with the day. This work might feel repetitive, and this is because it is! Changing and reprogramming long-term behavior patterns require repetition and practice in order for them to be sustainable.

The decision is yours to take – You are the CEO of your life.

1.

THE FUTURE

I t is important to think ahead. Having dreams and making goals is motivating and energizing, and offers you focus and vision.

Later in life it is wonderful to be able to start thinking about what you can give back. This is one of the many reasons I feel getting older is actually quite nice. The drive to achieve is replaced with giving back, helping, and supporting others.

Thinking about the future, dreaming, and having goals helps you connect with yourself, get in touch with what is in your heart, find your inner desires. You can take stock of how well your life is serving you by taking some time to reflect on what is working and what is not working. I suggest writing these thoughts down. When something is on paper it seems to carry more weight for being real. Schedule time for yourself when you know you will not have any interruptions and think about how you are feeling, what you like, what you do not like about yourself, what comes naturally to you, and what is more difficult.

With this information in mind, base your goals and dreams on who you are, taking your natural talents and characteristics into consideration. You will feel motivated and energized to pursue your dreams. Sometimes a dream is pursued and yet many obstacles keep cropping up. To me this is a good opportunity to reassess if the goal is still one I can connect to. The actions you take, or avoid, offer clues. When obstacles keep appearing I refer back to everything I know is really important to me (i.e., my core values). I also remind myself of what my strengths and weaknesses are. I know what to look out for when it comes to my weaknesses. I explore all this in order to make sure this is something I really want to do and not something I think I should be doing.

I find there are ideas, wishes, goals that are just not meant to be. Maybe not at all or maybe the timing is wrong. With this approach you can course correct and reset your goal achievement strategy.

Goals are usually around:
- What you want to be
- What you want to do
- What you want to have

A goal is not a target but a desired outcome you wish to be realized. Once you have achieved it you will have enhanced your life in some way.

CLEAN UP YOUR LIFE FOR A BETTER FUTURE

Dealing with problems requires being practical and realistic.

If your life feels like it is a mess and you are ready to take some action, there are many different approaches to consider. Support from a professional or wise friend, meditation, spiritual beliefs, sometimes even just taking a "time out" holiday can help. Find the one that suits your personality and lifestyle best. You are looking to be more grounded in the present, calmer and therefore having more clarity. You are more likely to stay on track with making the necessary changes with a realistic clear mind.

Imagine a ladder; each rung on the ladder represents the changes necessary. Accept the fact that you will get to the top one step at a time, not in one fell swoop. Make sure you break this "clean up plan" down into smaller steps and take one at a time.

To get yourself on track to feeling better and living the kind of life you wish for, ask yourself these six questions:

1. How motivated and ready are you to clean up your life? This means you will need time for yourself and to be dedicated to this project.
2. Find some time that allows you to stop, slow down, and sit quietly.
3. To narrow down where to start, think about what is going on: What specifically is giving you this feeling of your life being a mess?
4. Is it one particular issue or several?
5. Which area of your life feels like a mess? Life at home, life at work?
6. What would make the biggest difference to you right now?

Remember that life is complicated and can be more difficult at times. Clearing your life up, getting rid of the deadwood, and finding your place of balance forms a wonderful basis. This is the best, most powerful place to work from and come back to when things are difficult. Being familiar with the feeling of being in balance allows you to know exactly what you want to get back to. This also offers you the goal to strive for. Life will always contain difficult times.

Refer to the Workbook section (Page 155) if at this point you wish to take a more in-depth look at where you stand in your life now and where you would like to be heading.

THE PRESENT

Eckhart Tolle refers to living in the now, which means being able to see and feel what your life is in the present moment. The present-day buzzword for this is to be mindful by practicing mindfulness.

Standing in a beautiful park, by a calming body of water, or attending your child's school play or other family event, and actually seeing the trees, feeling the flow and energy of the water, enjoying the play or event while feeling joy instead of being lost in your thoughts is experiencing the now, the present moment, being mindful.

Thoughts can propel you into an entirely different location even if you are not there physically. It seems odd that we do not just naturally live in the now. After all, almost everyone would agree that the present moment, the now, is all we have. The fact remains that most people do not live in the now and have to learn how to do so. When you concentrate more on the present, life becomes more relaxed and enjoyable. This becomes a powerful technique to step out of stress. Everybody spends a fair amount of time focusing on work, planning schedules, gaining understanding, engaging in problem-solving, etc., all of which of course involve forward thinking. During your downtime, or as my son refers to it, "powering down," the ability to enter the now is vital. Otherwise life passes you by.

Be patient, because giving yourself to the present takes a lot of practice and time. Eventually you will appreciate the power that you gain with this ability to experience the moment.

Refer to the Workbook section on The Present (Page 163) if at this point you wish to take a more in-depth look at where you stand in your life now, in a sense to give yourself a reality check.

BE IN THE MOMENT, IN THE NOW

There are wonderful books, classes, films, talks, workshops, DVDs, magazine articles, conversations, coaches, and therapists teaching the importance of being in the moment, staying in the now, and going with the flow. But how do you really do this?

It seems odd that we do not just naturally live in the now. After all, almost everyone would agree that the present moment, the now, is all we have. The fact remains that most people do not live in the present moment and have to learn how to do so.

Reasons to master living in the moment:
- You receive instant relief from stress
- You are able to manage fears better
- You become calmer. A sense of calmness enters if you stop to take a few breaths. Focusing on your breathing returns your mind to the present moment, away from your thoughts.
- You feel stronger and some of your personal power returns. You feel stronger because you took charge of the moment. This offers the feeling of having influence and consequently strength.

Our minds tend to take us to places and times that are not real. What might be real in that moment is a beautiful tree right in front of you. The boss that was rude to you earlier in the day is no longer standing there or even still in the same room as you!

The gain of living more in the present is that life becomes more relaxed and enjoyable. It becomes a powerful technique enabling you to step out of stress.

Steps to practice being in the moment:
- *Realize and accept that you are free to choose in each and every moment.* You can choose not only what you do, but also what you

think. This awareness is the first – and often the hardest – step to integrate into daily life. It is, however, an important truth.

- *Raise your awareness to where your thoughts are taking you.* Perhaps you find yourself lost in a thought relating to a future or past event while you are actually taking a wonderful walk.
- *When you catch yourself no longer being "there," remind yourself that you are free to choose in that moment what you think or do.*
- *Make up your mind where you want to be.* Do you want to be enjoying your walk and taking in what you see, breathing the fresh air, or do you want to be lost in something that is truly not relevant to the time and place you are in at that moment?
- *Find a way – a little trick or an image – that will support you in breaking your thoughts at that moment.* Some people imagine putting their thoughts into a cloud that is passing by, or into a boat that they then push away from shore. Really negative thoughts can be placed into a building that you then blow up! Another way is to pinch yourself or turn in a circle a few times. Find something that suits your personality.
- *Take a few breaths and focus on exactly where you are and what is going on.*

By practicing these steps, you can slowly teach yourself how to stay in the moment, or at least how to bring yourself back from where your mind has taken you. This applies to all actions and thoughts. You may be at work, getting on with your job and all is fine. However, you find yourself lost in the pain of something that happened that morning with your partner. Ask yourself how that pain is relevant to the present moment at work. Focus on what is actually happening right around you in that moment. Tell yourself it is all right to resolve the issue around the pain at its appropriate time, e.g., when you see your partner or get a chance to call.

Be patient because this takes a lot of practice and time. Eventually you will appreciate the power that you give yourself with this ability to be mindful.

I was working with one of my clients, whom I will call Elaine, who had the tendency to react, motivated by past emotions. Our focus was to bring her to a place of acting, rather than reacting. Here is what Elaine felt she achieved from learning to put herself back into the now.

1. I am able to solve problems more easily because I only have to deal with the one actually on the table in front of me. I know that future problems (projections) will be solved at that moment, at that time. With this separation, I am able to worry less about the future, knowing that problems will be solved when they occur.

2. With this way of looking at things and problem solving, I feel a sense of freedom and can enjoy the day more – even if it is a difficult one. The load is not so heavy because I am only carrying the load of the present day.

3. Feeling freer gives me strength, which makes me ready for everything that happens in the moment.

4. I have more time. It seems that not wasting time by worrying about what might be, or feeling the emotions of what was, I create space. Space equals more time to me.

5. I enjoy my own company more. This makes me happier.

6. It has been hard and takes practice, but it is well worth it to feel the way I do now.

By mastering the art of living in the moment, you are taking good care and being very kind to yourself. That alone should make it worth the effort.

Dilgo Khyentse Rinpoche was quoted as saying: "Do not encumber your mind with useless thoughts. What good does it do to brood on the past or anticipate the future? Remain in the simplicity of the present moment." Wise words to remember, don't you think?

YOUR INTUITION — THAT GUT FEELING OR INNER VOICE

We all know that feeling of "knowing" we should not be following through with a decision, but we go on and do it anyway. This can be as simple as turning right when driving somewhere when we feel that turning left is really what we should be doing. You know it is wrong because it does not feel right on some level, yet your brain overrules that feeling with mind chatter or you allow someone else to influence you.

Your intuition – your gut feeling – is always there to let you know when you are not being true to yourself or to your soul. It does this by making you uncomfortable with what is going on, and this is a sensation that most often arises in the gut. You are born with an unimpaired intuition, a pure one, like the instincts animals have. Somehow while growing up, this unimpaired intuition becomes suppressed, blocked by something, and overruled by the mind.

Lessons to be learned about intuition are:
- While growing up and being influenced all around us we take on the values of our parents, our siblings, our friends, our teachers, the media, or of what "they" say (whoever "they" may be). This is social conditioning. The result is that the natural access to your intuition becomes blocked. It is best to accept that it is all a part of life and happens to most of us.
- At some time or another, most of us get to a point in life when we realize we are not quite happy, content, at peace, and satisfied enough to leave things as they are, and we begin to ask questions. These lead – without fail – to change. They are grounded in your intuition, which has reached a level of saturation with being overruled by the mind. Your intuition and soul want to

be heard to put you either on track or back on track with your purpose.

- You reach a level of maturity when you have the courage to be more true to yourself, regardless of the consequences. These consequences invariably are what others might think, how others might react, how others will be affected, what all these changes might mean in our day-to-day life, and so on. All humans resist change as much as they desire it. Change takes courage and motivation.

It is very important to know and accept that everybody has an intuitive sense. Think of that gut feeling of simply knowing something is not right even while you go on and do it anyway. This "knowing" is your intuition, your inner voice. Its main job is to keep you safe and put you on track if you get sidetracked from the wishes, desires, values, and path of your true self.

How can you tell when your intuition is giving you guidance? One of my father's favorite phrases was "When in doubt... out." The "doubt" in my opinion is your intuition attempting to tell you something, or maybe even warn you relating to the decision you are about to make. I also love the line in the movie Ronin when Robert de Niro's character says, "When there is a doubt, there is no doubt!"

Sometimes you will only listen to your gut feeling once your mind has exhausted itself of its rationalizations. Your mind prefers things to remain the same so it will happily deliver all the reasons not to listen to your inner guidance. The mind speaks loud and often with harsh words, rationalizing its suggestions based on past events. It finds ways to keep you behaving the same way as ever.

The inner voice, your intuition, does not use words to communicate with you. You will know when it is speaking. You will feel it in your gut or your heart. However, to hear it you will need some quiet time, away from mind chatter. This space allows your gut feeling to sense what is right and communicate this to you. I get my best intuitive "hits" in the early morning hours. Being an early bird I love the quiet and calm before the world starts ticking. It is at this time when my mind is quieter, without any specific focus and there is enough space and clear connection between my mind and intuition. My best ideas come when the two are working together! I really feel at my full power.

One of the best pieces of advice anybody can offer is to sleep on it: not to react to something but to wait until it is right for you to act upon it. If you put a problem in an imaginary box the night before going to sleep and upon waking ask yourself what is the right thing to do, the answer will come from your intuition instead of being smothered by the day's events.

When following your intuitive insight, a sense of calm and relaxation will be with you. If the mind offers a solution that is not right, however, you will probably remain feeling a little uncomfortable, if not tense, depending on the importance of the matter in question.

The more you listen to your inner voice, the more it can develop. It is like a muscle that can become stronger. Learn to trust it.

Your intuition is powerful. If you listen to it, allow it to guide you, it has the ability to shape your reality. When meeting new people, you have an intuitive sense about them that lets you know when it is appropriate not to trust a person or situation. You can attempt to rationalize all you like but you will probably later find that this did not make a difference. Your intuition is your soul's guidance system and trumps all.

Becoming acquainted with your inner voice will move you closer to yourself. This, of course, offers wonderful chances to make choices based on what your life means to you. The benefits of living your life while basing your actions not only on your mind's wisdom, but also that of your soul, will be immensely rewarding. In my coaching practice I find repeatedly that connecting people to their true self is what makes the biggest difference. Once you are living in that place of authenticity, most large problems become much smaller and are more easily coped with because you have your inner guidance system to accompany you. You are never alone.

PATIENCE

The thoughts relating to patience here are related to personal development.

Patience is important when you are changing any patterns – thinking or behavior – that have been part of you for a while. It is wise to manage your expectations when it comes to how long an overall shift could take. Wanting it all too quickly leads to disappointment and disappointment often leads to a lack of motivation to keep working at it.

Patience can be defined as the ability to delay gratification and be okay for things to happen in their own time. This is a good trait to have, not only during your personal growth and development but also in life.

Once you are motivated to make a change it is important to know that success will come if you allow yourself time to practice the new behavior. This requires you to be patient with yourself which means you are showing yourself respect and compassion. This in turn rewards you with feeling good, focused and motivated. Self-respect and compassion enhance your self-confidence which raises your self-esteem.

Think in terms of patience being like a muscle that needs to be exercised in order to become stronger.

Impatience with your personal growth and development is self-sabotage so remember: patience really is a virtue.

3.

THE PAST

E verybody has a past. Without it we would not be alive or be who we are. Living in the past, however, robs you of the present. Carrying the past with you is not only a load of emotional baggage to drag along, but it can also block you from seeing what the present has to offer.

In my coaching practice, exploring some of this baggage is sometimes necessary to find out what exactly my clients are still hanging on to. Pain that remains should be healed, and beliefs that sabotage with constricting behavior patterns should be replaced by healthier ones. If you carry any *I have to* or *I should's* it is best to find a new more positive perspective. New, exciting, energizing people and things can appear in the space created by leaving behind all that no longer serves your present-day life. Sometimes people, things or opportunities appear out of nowhere!

Allowing part of your life to be lived in the past means you are compromising what you could have in your life now. Enjoy the memories, allow them to energize you and offer you creativity, but do not hang on to anything no longer of value – and in fact irrelevant – to your present-day life.

Issues related to unhealed wounds that carry a lot of pain are topics that can be addressed with one of the traditional therapies, for example psychoanalysis or hypnotherapy. I have benefited from cognitive analytical therapy and cognitive behavioral therapy as well as hypnotherapy. Letting go of the past while looking toward the future is rejuvenating.

LETTING GO OF THE PAST

The best place to start is by understanding what you can gain from letting go of the past. We tend to focus on what might be lost and frequently overlook what the benefits of taking this step are. Try to imagine a life already free of the images and thoughts from the past inhibiting you in the present. Imagine how it would feel if you maintained positive memories, ones that energized you rather than ones that drained you. Sometimes you may be so entangled in old problems that you cannot see the changes that are necessary to make your life better. For this you will need to clear out the deadwood and make space for the new.

You know that the past is the past; nevertheless, you are still caught up in it through strong emotions. Intellectually you understand what is going on but somehow your emotions do not.

Consider the following exercises to release the now irrelevant emotions. These emotions can be anything from pain, frustration, and anger, to confusion and disappointment, even ones that have no name!

1. *Cry it out.* According to Dr. William Frey II, crying away your negative feelings gets rid of harmful chemicals that build up in your body due to stress. Let go by allowing them to wash over you. It might feel horrible, but you will be relieved and peaceful afterward. Let go by really feeling your way into the emotion. If you stifle your feelings, they may be expressed in a different way and may affect everyone around you. The point is that you have to feel an emotion fully in order to free yourself of it.

2. *Express your feelings through a creative outlet.* A favorite of mine is to write the feelings down on paper. Once you have finished,

scrunch it up, rip it to shreds, or cut it into pieces. Then take the paper (or in my case the little pieces left!) outside and burn them in a safe place. (Burning is a good idea as long as this process is not a fire hazard. Use a fireplace or a barbecue.) Otherwise, ripping up or cutting is just as effective. As it goes up in smoke watch the slips of paper disappear into nothing. Imagine your negative feelings flowing away with the smoke, or in the case of ripping/cutting, reducing the size of the emotion. It feels wonderful!

3. *Metaphorically throw your feelings away:* Picture a house in your mind where you place the emotions, then blow it up with imaginary dynamite. This one works best if the emotion you have is anger. The feelings can be placed on a cloud and you can watch them drift away.

4. *Choose the action or visualization that works best for you.* I like throwing rocks into the lake, each one symbolically representing something I am letting go of.

5. *Remind yourself physically.* When your mind takes over by flooding you with negative thoughts, wear a rubber band on your wrist and gently flick it. This trains your mind to associate that type of persistent negativity with something unpleasant.

Once you have managed to heal some old wounds and move forward with less baggage from the past you will feel energized, more motivated, and stronger in the present.

Through the Workbook starting on page 155 you will explore the past more deeply.

YOUR THOUGHTS LIMIT OR EMPOWER YOU

As Henry Ford so wisely stated: "Whether you believe you can or cannot – Either way you are right." In other words, if you think and believe something to be true, then it is your truth. If you think you cannot do something... you cannot, and most probably will not even try. If you believe you can figure something out... most probably you will find a way. Your beliefs can be negative or positive, therefore they can limit or empower you.

If you feel there is a better version of yourself, then examine if it is a thought/belief that is holding you back from reaching your potential.

It could be anything from:
- I do not know how
- I do not have any support
- I do not know where to start
- I am uncertain about this

Beliefs are thought patterns, evaluations, opinions, judgments, and generalizations that you hold about yourself and others. These beliefs can stem back to your early formative childhood years and could have been stored there in your unconscious mind ever since. They can also be from experiences as a teenager, young adult, or adult. Experiences with your parents, relatives, siblings, teachers, and friends can affect your beliefs. Your social environment, traumatic experiences, media influence, or repetitive experiences add to the collection of information that forms these beliefs, be it negative or positive.

The first law of perception is that the eyes see but it is the mind that tells you what you see. One of the reasons the mind tells us what we see, or perceive, is that the underlying beliefs tend to make us look for certain things. For example, a cynic will see what he or she is looking for just as much as an optimist will see what he or she is looking for. Each chooses their experience from their beliefs. When you believe something to be true, naturally you act as if it is. You bring on what you expect. (Think placebo effect.) If you continually act in ways that support negative beliefs, negative events tend to materialize. People are like magnets – you attract what you believe.

To unlock your potential and be the person you know you are, these limiting beliefs should be replaced with positive, empowering ones.

Holding on to self-limiting patterns ensures that your potential can never be reached. When you believe you can... you find the way forward, one small step at a time. Once you are wired with positive, empowering beliefs, you automatically set goals you know you can achieve and therefore are successful in reaching them. You can have empowering beliefs that will encourage growth, which leads to change and a happy, successful, and fulfilling life.

LIMITING THOUGHTS AND BELIEFS

I have witnessed all too often with friends, family, clients, and of course in my own life, how easy it is to feel you are going in circles or banging your head against the same wall. It feels like your ability to move forward is blocked. You keep ending up in the same place, repeating the same patterns.

The behavior keeping you going in circles is often fed by a limiting belief. This limiting belief drives your behavior to repeat patterns which hinder your growth and development. The specific disempowering and limiting belief is best uncovered and dealt with.

A coaching client never quite achieved the goals he set himself. Despite taking proactive steps, he still ended up going around in circles. On one level he believed in the success of his project, yet deep down inside a little voice kept repeating, What's the point? You won't really succeed. In his case, the little voice was his impatience, which kept him going around in the same circle. Instead of taking a little extra time and dealing with issues that appeared, he would push forward, overlooking them until they had accumulated to a point where they blocked the success of the project. We reframed his limiting belief "Things have to happen quickly in order to be successful," to a healthier one. "Being patient does not mean I will not succeed." The result was more patience, which led to a successful outcome of his project.

Think in terms of getting the virus out of the software!

Steps to dismantle limiting beliefs:
1. *Motivation* – Explore how you will benefit from working on changing this. Make a list of what you have to gain.

2. *Awareness* – The next step is to uncover specifically which thought keeps cropping up that limits you. Write it down.

3. Examine whether this thought is in your best interest; is it actually true? If not, *choose* to change it.

4. *Reframe* – Ask yourself what the opposite of this thought is. Find a sentence that will be a) easy to remember and b) feels right. Do not try to fool yourself, so keep it realistic; you want to believe that you can do this. As an example: if you keep thinking you do not know how to do something, consider "If I did know how, what would I be doing differently?"

5. Write the reframed thought down.

6. Consider what you can do to remind yourself of the new reframed belief.

   How can you help yourself in the moment when the limiting belief kicks in?

   It often helps to read it in the mornings and evenings. Do whatever you can think of that will be supportive to you. One of my clients put fresh flowers on her desk as a reminder of what she was practicing.

7. Seek support if you are struggling; this is not always easy to shift on your own.

8. Know that "If you believe you can or cannot, you are right!"

4

CHANGE

Thoughts about change usually only occur when life no longer offers you the feeling of being satisfied. These thoughts can also emerge when things are basically all right but there is room for improvement. The difficulty frequently lies in finding out specifically what you can improve, what you should move on from, and/or what you should let go of.

Change is not easy or simple. It can only really occur if you are ready to take action. Research shows 90% of the strategies designed for change assume people are ready to take action and follow through.

In reality only 20% of the people already involved in some process of change are actually ready to take action. This helps explain why so many people who attempt to succeed with New Year's resolutions are doomed to fail. Often in the workplace and relationships a change of behavior is suggested, however, if you are not convinced this is necessary you are more likely to fail at completing the process.

Change is all around you and constant, be it in your private life, surrounding society, or at work. It is not always easy, takes time, and requires new skills and behavior. Even if you know changing is for the better, it might provoke fear. I like to think of the process as climbing a ladder – take one small step at a time at whatever speed suits you, your lifestyle, and your personality. You will reach the top provided you try not to rush it. Be patient and kind with yourself along the way.

Awareness that things can be different is the first step to change. Once you are truly aware of this you have already taken the first step. This is to say that small steps are more realistic, valuable, and above all, fit more easily into day-to-day life.

Once you have made up your mind that "something has to change," this is a good time to start. If your motivation comes as a result of trying to please someone else, then realize that you might not succeed. Do this for yourself, not for someone else.

Engaging the support of a friend or life coach for encouragement, motivation, understanding, and accountability can be helpful and will increase your chances of success. Specifically *how* your support person can be helpful varies from individual to individual, so make sure you communicate clearly how you need him or her to be.

For your brain to make the changes and rewire itself it will need to experience success, which will keep you motivated. It has been scientifically proven that the brain can rewire itself, thereby changing thinking patterns.

Success builds motivation and creates momentum. Handling any small setbacks – which are to be expected and are part of the process – becomes easier if at the same time you are experiencing small successes.

So remember:

- Be happy with small steps and small successes. This is what keeps you motivated.
- Experiencing reward is necessary.

Dopamine, better known as the "happy hormone," plays a vital role to your levels of motivation. In order for you to feel and stay motivated, a steady stream of dopamine released into the brain is necessary. The brain will release dopamine if there is even just a 50% chance of success. You can help release it while being creative, with exercise, listening to music, touch and massage, meditation, and through a balanced diet. There is lots of valuable information about this you can research.

Believe in the steps you are taking – know that handling yourself better does lead to change and a better future.

The most successful way to approach changing a behavior pattern is to:

- *Acknowledge* that things can no longer stay the same.
- *Accept* that it is possible to do things differently.
- *Take the time* to gather the necessary knowledge, insight, and support.
- *Raise your awareness* of how your life will change in a positive way by making this change. Making a pro and con list tends to help.
- *Decide what steps* need to be taken to move in the right direction.
- *Recognize* any denial or disempowering, defensive, or self-sabotaging behavior.
- Understand and accept that you and your life are worth this effort.
- Recognize and work through the obstacles and possible self-sabotage routines that appear.

Get back on track if there was a hiccup or pause. Catch yourself, and recognize when an old habit has found its way back in. Remind yourself of what and how you want to be; reflect to find out what happened to let the old behavior/thinking in. Reassess and restart.

Remember experiencing success is vital for a change to take full effect. Be integrated in your behavior and become part of the "new you."

Keep yourself motivated and know it is okay to make mistakes along the way.

That is not to say you cannot make a change with a decision and follow through (e.g., stop smoking, change your eating habits, stop using certain words, etc.). That is entirely possible. Some, however, take a little more time and practice.

Coaching is about behavior change, which is the reason I am so passionate about it. Although change takes time, it is achievable. In my practice I have learned that when I am interviewing potential clients, if during this chat I hear "Yes, but..." often, I know the first part of our coaching relationship will be focused on establishing and anchoring our work with their motivation to change and follow through.

When you no longer remember how you were before, that can be seen as a measure of success.

BREAK THAT BAD HABIT!

Breaking habits can be difficult. "You have to keep doing it until you can't do it anymore!" – this was a phrase my best friend used to say every time I moaned about how fed up I was with myself for re-peating the same pattern. One of the habits I was delighted to eventu-ally break was always taking better care of others than I did of myself. I now smile that my passion is actually helping and supporting oth-ers with coaching. The difference is I no longer neglect myself, or my needs, and disrespect my values. In the past I had all good intentions, then something would happen and I would fall off the track. This con-tinued until one day these wise words rang true: "I had done it until I couldn't do it anymore." I was finally in the place of being ready to make a change.

Once you have reached that point, one of the most important as-pects of breaking a habit is to make sure you have found exactly the right amount of motivation, which will support you along the way. It is probable that as a normal human being you will make mistakes. This is the time to remember that tomorrow is a new day, and you can start again, having re-motivated yourself.

Schedule some time, grab pen and paper, and explore the following questions. This will help you get motivated to start and provide you with information about yourself you might not have known or have forgotten.

- Imagine how it will feel once you have changed this habit. Think of the things you would be doing differently.
- Allow yourself to take time for a new behavior to be in place. These things do not happen overnight.
- Acknowledge that you have taken the first and most often hardest step. You have accepted that something can be done.

To help start breaking a bad habit ask yourself:
- How would you prefer to be?
- How will you feel about yourself?
- For motivation consider: What will you gain? What will you lose?
- Make two lists
- Examine what exactly you can start doing differently – design your action step.
- Which one of these actions will give you the best results, is most realistic, is possible, and is in your power?
- What is the *best first step*?
- How can you proceed to take this step? And when?
- Follow through, taking small steps at a time, and be kind to yourself during this process. Practice and repetition will lead to success.
- If you feel some support would be helpful or you feel like you need to discuss your thoughts with someone, who you can contact?

This can be a long or short process depending on the habit you are looking to break. Allow yourself to make mistakes even if you feel you are taking one step forward and two steps back at times. Keep your motivation in check and stay on track. If you practice and repeat the new behavior, you will succeed. One important piece of information I took away from working with a therapist many years ago was to allow myself not to always get it right straightaway.

WORK OR FAMILY HIJACKED YOUR LIFE?

It can happen without you even noticing that your life no longer feels as though it is your own. Overwhelming work demands, busy family schedules, even modern technology seem to add stress by making you accessible all the time. All this becomes a priority, while you and your own personal life, values, beliefs, thoughts, wishes, and dreams come in second place, if not third.

Your attention ends up being stretched in too many directions with no time left to think about yourself.

Ask yourself the following questions when you are ready to start getting your life back:

1. What happened to trigger this feeling?

   For example, did you change jobs, get a promotion, move to another house or even a different country, and fall out of your old routine?

2. Which part of you feels the most neglected?

   Think of all the essential parts that make up a successful life:

   - Health
   - Career
   - Purpose/Meaning
   - Finances
   - Home environment
   - Friends and family
   - Recreation and fun
   - Personal growth and development

   Make a list. Writing things down rather than just thinking about them makes a big difference. If necessary, ask your friends or family to help you by telling you what they observe is important to you. They can often see more because they are looking in from the outside.

3. Once you have your list ask yourself what you would do if you only had one choice; which area would you put all your energy into? Where is the best place to start? What would make the biggest difference to you now? If you only had time to do one thing differently, what would that be? Would it be getting some exercise, chatting with a friend, cleaning your home, or becoming a little more organized in an area that is important to you?

4. If you are not sure you will stay motivated to follow through, ask yourself:
   What price am I paying for neglecting this? Is my health, family, soul, own personal growth, or home suffering? The answers to these questions are good to note somewhere. When you lack motivation refer back to these answers.

5. In order to take action, decide where can you find time. Get up ten minutes earlier? Could you spend a few hours over the weekend focusing on yourself?

6. Maybe you need to say no to someone or to a situation? For example, saying no to an offer to go out when in fact what you need is time for yourself.

7. For support: Who could you talk to? Whose assistance would be helpful?

Allow yourself time and patience to turn this around. This is a very important point – change/transformation takes time in order to be sustainable!

Be kind to yourself as you learn to make yourself a priority. You might have to start with only five minutes per day or every other day until slowly you carve out more and more time for yourself. Aim for thirty minutes per day.

Accept that if you do not take care of yourself, nobody else will.

It is the most empowering feeling to know you can take the best care of yourself. Your self-esteem will love this.

BE KIND TO YOURSELF

As an independent adult you have become the "Chief Executive Officer" of your life. You can live your life... it does not have to be living you!

In the moments when you are feeling stressed, one of the simplest yet most effective ways to reduce the tension is to spend some time doing something that involves your senses.

Whenever possible take a break from technology, even if only for one hour. If that is not possible, try ten minutes during which you turn off your computer, your phone, TV, etc. If you cannot go outside, then look out of the window at the sky. Regardless of the weather, the sky can be inspiring and energizing.

To connect to that sense of well-being:
1. Think about what exactly it is you are doing when you feel happy, fulfilled, at peace, nurtured.
2. If you cannot come up with an answer, think back to a day or event that you enjoyed, that made you feel good.
3. Use your imagination and senses to remember what that felt like, and bring up any images you have of that day.
4. What can you draw from that feeling now? Might you be able to do it again? For example, were you outside, talking with a friend, eating something wonderful, sitting still, appreciating a view? If it were not possible to do any of those things right now, what is possible right now that would be good for you?
5. Can you do something creative or something you do not normally do or have time for? Take a bath, connect with a friend or family?
6. Even five minutes will make a difference. You do not need to have all day to be kind to yourself.

7. Do one thing; however small, try to do this daily and then build on that.

If you are at work do whatever is possible and realistic.

Once you have started experiencing how even a small step can support you and make you feel more grounded and calm, you will want more!

FEELING POWERLESS AND LIKE A VICTIM?

If you're feeling helpless and unsure of what to do, and powerless over the immediate situation, you may feel like a victim of the circumstance. Maybe you feel like you have been treated badly or unjustly. Wherever this stems from, it can make you feel disheartened with what is going on in your life. Remember, you can always start on a new path with a new approach.

With reference to my own personal growth and development: I am fortunate to have met Jane Long many years ago in a pottery class when I was living in Dorset, England. I met her at just the right time in my life. By this I mean: *When the pupil is ready, the master appears* (unknown). I was ready for a new path and open to learning about new approaches to life. Jane became my emotional therapist to help me move forward to a better place. She loved sending me away from our sessions burdened with things to read. I used to moan and groan all the way as I was still hoping there was an easy quick fix option.

When it comes to personal growth, there is no easy option. You need introspection, learning, reframing, time, patience, practice, and to heal any wounds keeping you stuck and holding you back.

One of the many papers Jane had given me was an excerpt from "Courage to Change," which turned out to be from the twelve-step program. It had a great impact on me and motivated me to get up off the floor and figure out how to makes some changes. When I read the first lines of the Victim Recovery description below I felt immediate relief. In the strangest way these words were like music to my ears as I could relate to *having become a doormat*. The relief was realizing that what I wanted to do was get up off the floor. All of a sudden I had a solution at hand. I already had taken the most difficult step, which was to get some support, so now I knew I was on the path to make necessary changes within myself.

Victim Recovery description (as quoted in "Courage to Change")

1. If I don't want to be a doormat, I have to get up off the floor. In other words, although I cannot control what other people say, do, or think, I am responsible for my choices.

2. Looking back, I can accept that plenty of unacceptable behavior was directed at me, but I was the one who sat and took it and often came back for more. I was a willing participant in a dance that required two partners. I felt like a victim, but in many ways I was a volunteer.

3. Today I know that I am not helpless. I have choices. When I get that old feeling that tells me I am a victim, I can regard it as a red flag, a warning that I may be participating (with my thoughts or actions) in something that is not in my best interest. I can resist the temptation to blame others and instead look to my own involvement. That's where I can make changes.

4. When I am troubled by another person's behavior, a complicated situation, or a disappointing turn of events, I do not have to take it personally. I am not a victim of everything that happens unless I choose to see myself that way. Though things do not always go my way, I can accept what I cannot change, and change what I can.

5. Perhaps I can take a different view of my problems. If I accept them at face value without taking them personally, I may find that they are not problems at all, only things that have not gone as I would have liked. This change of attitude can help free me to evaluate the situation realistically and move forward constructively.

6. Blaming my discomfort on outside events can be a way to avoid facing the real cause – my own attitudes. I can see myself as a victim or I can accept what is happening in my life and take responsibility for my response. I may be guided to take action

or to sit still, but when I listen to the guidance of Higher Power, I will no longer be the victim of my circumstances.

Decide to take responsibility for the quality of your life. Once you start to take responsibility for your decisions, actions, and consequences you will start feeling a sense of power you will not have felt while in the victim role. If helpful to you, I recommend you think about who can offer you some support and how exactly they can help. You might ask a friend for their open and honest support and feedback or consider working with a professional therapist or qualified and experienced life coach.

5

PERSONAL POWER COMES WITH PERSONAL DEVELOPMENT

According to the Business Dictionary personal power is "Influence over others, the source of which resides in the person instead of being vested by the position he or she holds." In my opinion personal power in nonbusiness language is the strength that lies within you. I feel I found my full personal power once I was aware and connected with my core values, had the life skills to handle difficult moments and situations, and had an influence on where my mind took me.

Personal power is composed of:
- Knowing who you are
- Being comfortable with yourself
- Knowing what is right and wrong, a personal code of ethics
- Being honest and trustworthy not only with others, but also with yourself
- Being dependable, again not only for others, but also for yourself
- Living your life from a place of integrity
- Handling your choices and their consequences, even the negative ones
- Knowing what you want, finding your way forward

- Knowing your weaknesses and your strengths
- Having an openhearted and nonjudgmental approach
- Taking responsibility for your actions and yourself

Personal power is an inner strength. Often you do not know you have it until it is needed. Personal power is acquired while growing up, through making mistakes, learning from these, making better choices, and trying new approaches. All of this contributes to personal growth and development – mastering oneself. This means living with respect for yourself, being true to yourself and to what is important to you. Once you know what it feels like to have your full personal power, it is hard to compromise that feeling.

What does it mean to have personal power?

People say, "You have power," or "Take your power back!" What are they talking about?

In my personal and professional opinion, you are in the place of knowing you can handle anything that is thrown at you – that is feeling your personal power. When obstacles pop up, your emotional triggers trip you up, or you are on the receiving end of someone else's emotions having been triggered and you handle it well and regain your sense of balance relatively quickly. When you feel in control of your emotions, your life, your path, and your way forward. Life is difficult yet you feel you can handle the obstacles – that is having personal power.

Here are a few examples of what it feels like to have your power:

- When you realize and accept you always have a choice. At any given moment you always have at least one choice: to do or not to do, to go or not to go, to say or not to say, to react or not to react. In other words, you can react in the moment and most probably regret it, or choose not to react, give it some time, and act on it a little later or even the next day.
- When you take responsibility for your actions. Regardless of whether the consequences of your actions were good or bad, you take responsibility for them and are comfortable enough to ask yourself: "What did I do, or not do, to help create this situation?"
- When your behavior allows you to sleep at night.
  You are not betraying yourself with the decisions you make or the actions you take. You are living from a place of integrity.

- When you are not living according to other people's standards or beliefs, but to your own.

  Know that when others have influence over you, you are allowing the volume of your power to be turned down.
- When you allow yourself to hear what your heart and soul have to say and you are not listening only to your mind.
- When you are strong enough not to play the blame game.

  Instead of concentrating on blaming something or someone when something has gone wrong, you ask yourself, "What can I do differently next time?"
- When you remember a thought only has power to the extent that you believe it to be true.
- If you do not believe something, it does not have any power. Beliefs that limit your actions are referred to as limiting beliefs or disempowering beliefs. These are thoughts that you treat as if they were facts, giving that thought your power and thereby limiting yourself.
- When you are not reacting – or behaving – in a manner motivated by your fears.

  For example, this could mean you choose to stay quiet rather than express yourself out of fear of losing something, or the fear of confrontation. There are many fears that drive our behavior. Recognizing what your fears are is vital in personal development. To recognize fears, observe what overwhelms, blocks you, gives you a stomachache, makes you think of all the reasons you cannot do something, or makes you go in circles always ending up in the same place.
- When you live in alignment with your personal core values, with respect for yourself, being true to yourself and what is important to you. To me this is one of the most important exercises to take my clients through. Reconnecting them with their

core values is a fabulous foundation for personal development. It can be quite magical.

With your personal power intact you can solve problems and achieve the results you want.

All of this contributes to personal growth and development – mastering oneself, not others. After giving your power away to others often enough, and putting yourself in a weak spot, you eventually learn how to make better choices. This is all part of life and its lessons.

CORE VALUES

Core Values are individual. They can be described as your code of ethics, your fundamental principles, your standards, or personal rules. I like to refer to them as the bricks you build your foundation on. Knowing what you truly value in life, what makes you feel fulfilled and gives you a sense of meaning, is an important part of your personal development.

Core Values are about YOU – not what society, the media, your education, your colleagues and friends or family deem as important, or of value, but what is important to you, what you value. Stress tends to set in when you are not treating these values with the respect they deserve.

Not respecting your core values means you are not respecting your true self.

In turn your self-esteem could suffer, which of course in turn decreases the quality of your day-to-day life. When the feeling of calm and peacefulness is present, the quality of day-to-day life high, you have the feeling of being a good person.

Caroline Myss, a five-time New York Times bestselling author and internationally renowned speaker in the fields of human consciousness and mysticism says: *"Being able to speak and live with the truth, your truth, means you have to become comfortable with having your power, be comfortable with all that is true about you, all that is beautiful about yourself, this is being okay with yourself."*

As an example of a core value, let's take "honesty," which happens to be one of my own core values. I imagine that everybody can relate to that feeling of not having been quite honest about something. The twinge felt deep inside, even if it was a "white lie" you still feel something, somewhere inside. If "honesty" is one of your core values, this means the need to not only be honest, but also to be treated with honesty. Should you find yourself not being totally honest about something, the lack of respect for this core value will leave a bad feeling inside, the feeling of not being true to yourself. The same goes the other way around. Finding yourself in the company of somebody you know or feel is not being honest with you creates an uncomfortable situation.

Living in line with your core values improves the quality of your day-to-day life, which in turn means being a better role model, parent, friend, co-worker, child, sibling, etc. It means you are maintaining your personal power. This applies to your personal life as well as your professional life. If you are not sure what all of your core values are, this is a wonderful exercise to do with a qualified life coach.

ALIGN YOUR LIFE WITH YOUR VALUES

Stress tends to set in when you are not treating these values with the respect they deserve. Not respecting them means you are not respecting your needs. In turn your self-esteem suffers, which of course in turn decreases the quality of your life. Honoring your values by making them a priority means you are choosing your behavior based on your personal code of ethics – your core values. In it is the choices you make and results in you being a better version of yourself. This in turn allows you to maintain personal power in your personal as well as professional life.

I find when stress kicks in it usually is because I am not paying enough attention to one of my core values. I figure out which one is being neglected followed by making choices around honoring it. In my case it can typically be overbooking myself. Being too busy means I lose the sense of calm and peace I value. I take some time to carefully explore my calendar and make the necessary adjustments between work and time-out. I manage to return to being more grounded and balanced, which is what honors my sense of calm and peace.

To be the best version of yourself here are six tips on how to align your lifestyle with your core values:

1. Recognize stress can be an imbalance between being too busy and time for relaxation.
2. Make sure you have some time to yourself, some downtime. Usually it is then when you have the space to recognize which of your values needs attention or maintenance.
3. Consider how you can give this value the priority it needs for you to feel better. What step needs to be taken. For example, if this is around "honesty," then narrow down what needs to be expressed to whom.

4. Find time to take this step – do not "squeeze it in or rush it."

5. Follow through with this action.

6. Acknowledge how you are feeling once you gave your value the attention it was lacking. In other words, celebrate the success no matter how small.

Honoring your values by making them a priority means you are choosing your behavior based on the right foundation, based on your personal code of ethics. You can only gain – it is a win-win!

6.

CHOICE

When it feels like you are pushing a large rock uphill or you keep walking into the same wall, it is difficult to realize that you have choices and there is more than one solution to any given problem.

Feeling there is no choice can make you feel helpless and blocked, as if you were at a dead end with absolutely no way out. Knowing there are choices gives you the sense that you have some influence over the outcome of a situation. Personal growth is ongoing throughout your life. The practical life skills you acquire along the way improve the quality of your day-to-day life. One important life skill to learn is how to find those choices when faced with a difficult decision.

Finding the alternative choices available to you means unleashing your creativity in some instances. Allow yourself to let your imagination run wild if appropriate, and above all do not forget to listen to that inner voice, your gut feeling, your intuition, if it is trying to speak to you about a choice you might have.

I help my clients to explore the choices and examine the consequences of each choice. Personally that is how I approach my issues/choices. I ask myself which consequences I want.

When life puts you into a situation where there is nothing you can do, this is the time to understand your choice in that moment is acceptance. This is indeed a choice, albeit a difficult one.

HOW TO DEAL WITH DIFFICULT DECISIONS

When you are faced with a difficult decision is a good time to remind yourself you always have choices. In the difficult moment, when emotions could be running high, it is hard to realize there is a solution to any given problem. It helps to acknowledge that having a choice is true for absolutely everything.

When it comes to things, people, and situations we cannot change, remember that we still have a choice as to how we react! This frequently relates to family and/or work-related interpersonal relationships. Do what is right for you, not what you think you should do to please others. Follow your intuition whenever possible. It is there to guide you in the right direction, however frequently its advice is ignored while the mind overrules.

To learn how to explore your choices, think of the situation you are facing and see if any of the comments below can be applied:

- Holding the situation in mind, consider to do, or not to do. By this I mean *I do nothing* or *I do something.* With this approach you already have figured out two choices available!
- If the issue is around communication: "I can choose to say something or to say nothing." Also, for your emotional reactions: "I choose to take offense in this situation, I choose not to react as though this were personal," or "I choose to say 'no' and set a boundary."
- You always have the option to leave things as they are and do nothing.
- Doing nothing means you have made the choice not to take action. Non-action is still a choice.
- If you choose to act, then accept it is you who has decided to do something.

- Either way there is always at least one choice.
- Think of a few scenarios to help you appreciate this is true (to have a cup of tea or not, to say something or not, to buy something or not, to leave a situation or not, to leave the relationship / location / job or not).

You might not always like the consequences of your choice, so think carefully before you take action.

Either way, you should always take responsibility for whatever choice you make.

Knowing how to explore what the various solutions/choices are is a life skill. With this skill, life becomes easier to keep in balance.

ACCEPT SOMEONE'S DECISION EVEN THOUGH YOU DO NOT UNDERSTAND IT

Someone makes a decision you simply do not understand. The consequences may or may not touch your life, involve you, or affect you. One way or another you cannot see what they are basing their decision on and the motivation behind it. This is the part that makes accepting their choice so difficult. I am going to break this down into two parts.

Part One: Empathy, compassion, and a better understanding Consider that:
- Everybody has the right to see life through his or her own eyes, the right to their own reality.
- Their reality will be based on experiences they have had so far in their life.
- These experiences will have formed their beliefs, values, goals, point of view, etc.
- Accepting and thereby respecting their choice means you are not judging them. Rather your approach is with compassion and empathy.
- With regard to judging others, ask yourself: "What gives me the right to judge someone?" or "What gives me the right to believe I know what is right for him or her?" If you think about this, it is quite presumptuous.

Part Two: Accepting a decision you might not understand.
- To truly accept means not to have any conditions attached to this acceptance. In other words, you accept unconditionally. As

mentioned before, each person has a right to his or her own reality to see life through his or her own eyes.

- Letting go of any conditions attached to your acceptance is how you set them free – "'allowing'" them to be themselves. This quote comes to mind: "If you love someone, set them free." Accept them and let them go.
- A few examples of conditions that sometimes interfere with acceptance: what *you* believe is right or how *you* think life is/should be, what decision *you* think is the best one. Basically any condition that involves a judgment based on your beliefs, values, and experiences is not respecting the other person's rights.
- To further help with acceptance ask yourself: "What will I lose if they do something I do not understand?" Consider this carefully, then ask yourself, "What will I gain if I accept their decision?".
- Finding the open-heartedness to look beyond yourself – this is setting someone free. Let them be who they are, follow their own path, be true to their own values. You will be surprised how good you will feel and how this strengthens your relationship with them. This is true for your personal life as well as your professional one.

Love / like them for who, how, and what they are. By doing this you are respecting their choices and decisions. Helping yourself reach the place of being able to respect their choices is also setting yourself free of judging people – a powerful skill to acquire.

CONTROL FREAKS, ALSO KNOWN AS MICRO MANAGERS

In the Oxford Dictionary, the definition of a "control freak" is "a person who feels an obsessive need to exercise control over themselves and others and to take command of any situation." The Merriam Webster dictionary says that a control freak is "a person whose behavior indicates a powerful need to control people or circumstances in everyday matters." One way or another, control freaks are not always easy to be around.

I understand this personality trait could stem from a chaotic childhood. Such experiences can make it hard for people to trust others or relinquish control to others. The fear of falling apart pushes them to control what they can. As their emotions are all over the place, they feel loss of control. For this reason, control freaks will micromanage whatever they can with the belief that this makes them strong. People who feel out of control tend to become controllers.

I imagine each and every one of us is a control freak, or takes on the behavior of such, at some point or another. The fear of failure is what makes it so important to control everything when you do not trust anybody else to do a good job.

One difficult aspect of being around a control freak is accepting that he or she does not understand how their behavior and choice of words affect the people around them. Another difficult aspect is not to take it personally. This behavior comes from deep inside and the person is actually quite unaware of the need to be controlling.

The attempts to control a situation or environment are intended to offer the controller a feeling of safety. This is a sign of low self-esteem.

One of the areas they often manipulate is conversation. A control freak is most comfortable if he or she decides what is talked about, for how long, and how deep or detailed a topic can be. This manipulation is achieved by constant interruption, finishing the sentence for the person, not listening with attention, doing distracting things like getting up and walking around, or even walking out of the room saying, "I am still listening." A control freak does not consider that he or she is being controlling, but is convinced his or her way is the right way. He or she will have an opinion about almost everything and will disagree with most suggestions that he or she does not instigate.

Controllers also control themselves; you might observe obsessive habits in them – whether in a private relationship or at work.

Here are helpful tips to consider when dealing with a control freak / micro manager:

- If someone dominates conversations, allow him or her to finish. Then, in a calm manner say, "I understand what you are saying and now I would like to express my thoughts."
- If someone continually gives you his or her advice by telling you exactly what you should be doing, again, in a calm manner say, "I value your advice, but I wish to consider my own thoughts on this matter as well."
- Your goal for establishing a healthier communication pattern with a control freak is to eventually "agree to disagree."
- Be as consistent as possible with the style in which you communicate. It will require patience and time, but it can result in turning the negative communication pattern into one that is more acceptable to you.
- Express yourself assertively without giving the person the feeling that you are telling him or her what to do. Never try to control a controller.
- Remain calm and be consistent with controllers. Getting angry does not achieve anything. Control freaks have no problem with arguments. In fact, they seek power struggles. Remember, in their minds the world should feel, think, and do what they deem is right.

- You can walk out of the room into a better space; they, however, are left with their issues, unless they seek support.

A control freak has the ability to bring you down a couple of notches and take the wind out of your sails. They can make people feel insecure. You may want to distance yourself if it is possible. If not, because the person is a member of your family or work colleague or boss, then consider what choices you do have based on the points raised above.

Raising your awareness to the fact that the person is micro-managing frequently already helps to make the situation easier to handle.

The benefits of establishing a manner of communication where you do not allow the control freak to rob you of your energy or drown you with negativity is that you become stronger, more assertive, and empowered.

In summary, here are helpful steps for handling the moment:

1. Acknowledge that you are in conversation with a control freak.
2. Whenever possible, buy yourself some time by taking a couple of deep breaths after excusing yourself for a minute. If you can leave the situation for longer, take a walk around the block to clear your head. Remind yourself that you are dealing with a control freak.
3. Accept that you are not going to be able to change how the person behaves or who he or she is. Maintain the focus on your reactions and communication style.
4. Remind yourself that you do not know what makes the control freak behave this way, so try not to judge them.
5. In conversations, listen without interrupting. Be calm and patient.
6. Express your own opinion/thoughts. Be assertive, but not aggressive.
7. Once the conversation is over, do something that will nourish you. This might be as simple as taking in a couple of deep

breaths and exhaling the negative energy the control freak brings along.

8. Accept that you handled the situation as best as can be expected and that it will take time and practice not to feel affected by a control freak/micro-manager's behavior style.

9. Being in the company of control freaks can feel like being with *Energy vampires*. Their ability to endlessly bring the attention back on to themselves is draining and exhausting. Knowing what to expect can help you choose how to interact and take care of yourself at the same time.

7.

LIFE SKILLS

Having life skills is essential to reaching your potential as well as feeling confident, strong, motivated, energetic, and content in the course of your life. They are the *software* you acquire along the way. You are born with the *hardware* – your body. Your behavior comes under the heading *software* because this can be changed, improved, modified, extended, or even deleted if necessary.

Many life skills are received in the home and at school while growing up. Others can be learned or enhanced by the school of life, friends, colleagues, courses, books, teachers, trainers, and coaches. The ones I come across often with my coaching clients are: interpersonal skills such as setting boundaries, prioritizing, time and stress management, better focus and increased motivation, to name a few. They can be defined as a group of cognitive and personal abilities that enhance your capability to lead a life in which you reach your potential. Every person has strengths and weaknesses.

Experiences, both positive and negative ones, are wonderful chances to learn from and grow. If you find yourself struggling with an issue, especially if it is a recurring one, this is the perfect time to learn from the situation – treat it as an opportunity.

Everybody goes through difficult phases, has obstacles to overcome and disappointments to heal. This cannot be avoided. How you cope is the key to making your life a success.

Not everybody has the same dream. Find your way forward based on your own strengths, values, dreams, and goals. The success of some people is not a matter of luck; they will have learned how to manage their life, and they will have acquired the software. Understanding that life is about change, which is inevitable, is one of the first steps on this ladder to the top! Your personal worth will benefit knowing you have the necessary skills in life to face everything that comes your way with confidence.

Life skills make a huge difference in how you handle the realities of day-to-day life.

Let us say you are in a checkout line in the supermarket. The cashier is clearly tired and in a mood – probably fed up of smiling all day while mostly being ignored or even treated badly. You are tired and hungry, want to get home, and you perceive the cashier's behavior as rude. In that moment you have a choice to react, judge the cashier, get annoyed and lost in your negative thoughts – they might even ruin the next twenty minutes for you. OR you can react with empathy by offering a few kind words. I like to think of the saying "If you see someone without a smile, give them yours." You will not only feel better, but you will also have touched someone else's life in a kind way. I think of this particular life skill as a) not being judgmental and b) having empathy. These are both valuable in life as well as at work. I am sure you can imagine an equivalent scenario in the workplace rather than in the supermarket.

Acquiring these life skills might feel time consuming. Once you have them, knowing when to reach for them will save you a lot of time you are now wasting by being emotional and stressed. It is wonderful to have an understanding of how things should be. Reality is normally a little different from what "should be!" Usually it is harder to deal with.

Emotions tend to enter when a difficult situation arises - at home or work. Once your emotions have been triggered, the issue is no longer just a rational one, it is now an emotional one. With emotions having kicked in, your cognitive resources are the first to be disrupted and depleted. This is a scientific fact. In other words, "you cannot think clearly" in the presence of your emotions.

This is the moment you will want to reach for the appropriate life skill which is to wait until your emotions are somewhat settled before you decide what comes next.

Life skills worth acquiring are coming up in the exercises to follow.

Self-Esteem

EXPLORING SELF-ESTEEM

Self-esteem is the overall impression you hold of yourself. This includes how much you value yourself and how you rate your abilities, as well as limitations. A low self-esteem will influence how you behave and what you achieve or do not achieve.

A healthy level of self-esteem offers a positive attitude, the capacity to be forward-looking with faith in your abilities to handle whatever comes your way.

When you have a healthy level of self-esteem you:
- Feel good about yourself
- Are confident and have the courage to change
- Have a positive attitude
- Value yourself
- Feel a sense of belonging
- Feel safe and empowered
- Tackle new challenges easily
- Can step out of your comfort zone when needed
- Believe you can achieve success
- Are able to create a good work/life balance

When you have low self-esteem you are:
- Self-critical
- Often apologetic
- Shy – which can sometimes show itself by being pushy and aggressive

You also:
- Avoid challenges
- Avoid eye contact
- Feel low energy

- Underperform at work and can be overlooked for promotions, etc.
- Find it difficult to ask for help
- Put the needs of others first – often neglecting your own needs
- Feel somewhat disempowered, maybe even in pain

Low self-esteem can be a significant obstacle that holds you back from succeeding in all aspects of life. Individuals and companies often do not consider that low self-esteem can hold a person back from advancing in life or career.

It is uncomfortable and painful not to feel good about yourself, to automatically focus on your limitations. Low self-esteem makes you vulnerable, sensitive to criticism and disapproval, anxious, frustrated, at times angry, and influences all areas of your life. Even people who are very sure of themselves will admit to having low self-esteem on occasion. Raising your self-esteem leads naturally to a place of power – you will have a positive feeling about your abilities, skills, and talents. It is worth taking the time to assess where you stand with yours.

BUILDING SELF-ESTEEM

Do you like what you see when you look into the mirror? If not, building your self-esteem will help change that. When self-respect and self-worth, both closely connected to your self-esteem, are improved, you will begin to feel increased self-confidence.

To establish a basis, make two lists:
- What you criticize yourself for
- What you praise yourself for

This alone is a great first step to working on your self-esteem level by raising your awareness to how things are in your life now.

There is no single way to build self-esteem. Some suggestions:
- Review the lists you made of what you criticize yourself for and what you praise yourself for. Ask yourself: How would it change my life if I were less critical of myself?
- Spend time exploring the lists. Familiarize yourself with how exactly you treat yourself. Are all these points really true?
- Self-respect is another good area to improve to raise your self-esteem.
- Taking care of yourself by having healthy, nurturing habits is essential. For example, eat healthily, look after your body, exercise, get fresh air, and make sure you like the environment in which you live.
- Raise your awareness and keep track of the negative statements you often say to yourself. Start making a list to refer back to.
- When you feel motivated to start changing how you speak to yourself choose one of the statements to start with. I suggest

the one that you feel would make the biggest difference to your daily life. If not that, then one you feel is the best place to start.

- Write the positive version down – put it on your fridge, bathroom cabinet, by your bed, on your desk – any place you feel you will see it frequently. Read it every time you see it. As an example of how to change a negative statement to a positive one: "I have no support" could be "There are people I can reach out to for support."

- Only wear clothes that make you feel good about how you look. Donate anything you do not really like, even if it is relatively new!

- Look through your photos and create a collage showing all the wonderful events you have enjoyed in your life. Pick the photos with people smiling or even better, laughing. I have a photo board in my kitchen and the criteria to be on the board is the people have to be smiling – giving off positive energy! I love looking at it while making my cup of morning tea. The smiling faces make me feel good.

- *"Act as if."* This is a wonderful tool to help you work out what specific steps you can practice while you are building your self-esteem. Ask yourself, "If I had high self-esteem, how would I behave or handle this situation?"

Remember success attracts success, just as negativity attracts more negativity. Surround yourself and mix with successful people, ones you admire, and ditch the energy vampires. A feeling of inspiration and motivation to create your own success will be the result. Your self-esteem can only increase if you stay open and dedicate some time to work on this. You are worth it; try to really see and feel that you are. Believe in yourself – you can do this by taking small, realistic steps that you can stand by and believe in. It is the baby steps that lead to success.

Emotional Strength

FEELING OVERWHELMED?

Coping mechanisms are essential when you feel overwhelmed. Here are tips to help you deal effectively with those initial difficult moments.

Important detail: All of these suggestions start with a couple of breaths.

- Stop what you are doing, sit down comfortably, take some breaths. While exhaling, imagine blowing the negative emotions out of your body. I like the visualization of blowing them out of the top of my head – it feels good!

Select the tips below that you are attracted to and have the time for.

- Reawaken your creative side. Nourish it by starting an enjoyable project or returning to a hobby. The best way to break your stress is by doing something that involves your senses. For example, you could draw an image on a piece of paper, bake something, do some gardening, rearrange a room, or an area of a room (a kitchen closet will do if you are not feeling too creative). Busying your hands allows your mind to focus on something other than the troubling negative thoughts. These kinds of activities are very grounding. As my mother always says: *Busy Hands are Happy Hands.*

- Whenever possible, use the word No. Remember that in order to say yes to something you might have to say no every now and then. Take the example of being invited to join some friends on the very night you were planning on staying at home for some downtime. In order to please them, you say yes. In this instance you chose to value your friends' wishes over your own. You said no to yourself while saying yes to them. In the end you have chosen to nurture them and not yourself!

- Meditate while sitting still or meditate while taking a walk by letting your mind take in all the wonderful sights nature has to offer. Focus on nature, what you see outside, and other peaceful images to push the other thoughts away. It is possible to find nature even if you live in the city. You can be indoors and look at the sky, or if you manage to go outside, consider how incredible nature always finds a way to bounce back.

- If you are able to, take a shower and feel how you can let the stress wash off and disappear down the drain. If you do not have enough time for a shower, wash your hands or take a quick walk outside. Feel the wind blow over you, or the warm sun shine on your face; even the rain can have a similar effect.

- Think about all of your good qualities. These might include your caring nature, your thoughtfulness, your ability to cook delicious meals, the love you have for others, being a good sibling, child, parent, or friend. Remind yourself of these qualities. Remembering these can offer you strength when you need it. Hold these good impressions for as long as possible. This will give you strength, if only for a minute or two. Reconnecting with your good qualities when you are feeling overwhelmed gives you a break from the negative feelings.

- Give yourself permission to take some time out to watch something funny, call somebody who makes you laugh, or nurture yourself with an activity that you know helps you relax. This might be taking a short nap, organizing a massage or Shiatsu, meditating, listening to music, watching a movie, or even sitting and doing nothing.

- Take three deep breaths, exhale slowly, and picture yourself surrounded by a golden bubble or golden egg. While exhaling, the tension is being expelled. Tell yourself that only good thoughts are allowed to come into the golden bubble or egg.

Choose whichever tip feels right. If necessary, make a note of it on your phone, computer, or notebook as a reminder until you reach for it naturally when overwhelm strikes.

FEELING REJECTED?

Everyone experiences two key feelings in life at some point or another: acceptance and rejection. Sometimes, you interpret the absence of one as being the other: if you are not accepted, you feel that you are being rejected and vice versa.

Being rejected, for whatever reason, is rarely an easy thing to experience. Rejection is a feeling of loss and comes in many forms. Here are a few reasons you may feel rejected: an idea you proposed was not accepted, a relationship you wanted has failed, you were turned down for a job you wanted.

Tips to help cope with those moments when you feel rejected:

1. Allow yourself to feel exactly what you are feeling. Cry if you need to or get angry if that is the emotion that surfaces. Whatever the emotion brewing inside, allow it to surface. Stay with your feelings and do not deny them. If this is not possible, then consciously park them on the back burner and address them later in the day.

2. To process what happened, focus closely on exactly what happened to make you feel this way. What did you experience that has left you feeling rejected?

3. Are you losing something by being rejected? Ask yourself what exactly you think you are losing, if anything? Be specific and honest with yourself. Only in this manner will you progress away from feeling rejected. Make a list of what you are losing, if only a mental one.

4. What will change in your life because of this loss? Is it an actual loss or perceived one? Maybe it is for the better?

5. Focus for a minute on what you *do* have rather than what you feel you *do not* have. What is working well?

6. For example, if you did not get the job, then might this be a chance to approach the job search differently? Is there something you can learn about yourself and how you are handling all of this? If you have been rejected in a relationship, what experiences can you take into the future? If your idea was rejected and you see that the idea was good but just presented badly or at the wrong time, how can it be improved upon?

7. Perhaps there is something to be gained as a result of what happened. Perhaps the situation was simply not right for you and a better opportunity will be available in the future.

8. Once you have processed the situation think about how you can move forward with your day. For example, take a walk or a bath, call a friend, or, even better, write down your feelings, thereby releasing some of those emotions.

9. Make your decision based on what will nourish you. Follow through with that walk, phone call, nap, bath, or even just take a couple of deep breaths if there is not time for any of the other options.

FEELING YOU FAILED?

In your perspective you feel you failed at something – this might not be at all true in someone else's eyes. It is easy to become swallowed up by your opinions. It is not a problem if they are positive ones. It is the negative ones that cause all the damage. Negative thoughts have so much power. They are the ones that can make you feel you failed.

Explore a change of perspective:
- Remind yourself that there is more than this one particular aspect that is not working out. Assess and bring your focus to what is good, what is working.
- Sometimes failing at something means it was not meant to be. Certainly not right now, perhaps never.
- Regard the situation as an opportunity to learn from. An opportunity to have tried something out, something that did not really feel right in the first place... and now you have your answer. It is not for you.

Personal growth and wisdom come from making mistakes, failing, looking at what went wrong, and identifying what could be learned from what just happened.

These questions might help:
1. Consider carefully what the specific points are at which you feel you failed.
2. What do you have to take care of? What kind of damage control is needed, if any?
3. What exactly have you lost?
4. Perhaps something was gained by not having succeeded. What could that be?

5. How can you start seeing this as an opportunity to learn?

6. If this is something you want to succeed at, how could you ap-proach it next time?

Reconsider how you view success. Not everything you do will work out the way you hoped. Sometimes the things you fail at are the ones that propel you to greater success. Encourage yourself to develop a view of success that does not easily lead to disappointment. How to overcome personal disappointment is one of the life skills invaluable to have. Being disappointed is never a pleasant feeling but a very real part of life.

What will it take to stand up, brush yourself off, and move on?

The choice is to dwell on the negatives or move on and see it as a learning experience.

- Imagine what it will be like when this no longer affects you.
- How much space will be freed up in your mind and in your heart?
- Consider what you lose by hanging on to feeling disappointed.
- What might you gain by letting go?
- How can you now slowly liberate yourself from this (which is now already in the past) and enjoy the present moment or day?

You will come across disappointment throughout your life. The measure of a successful person is one who handles disappointment with grace and dignity.

Energy vampires – How to deal with people who drain your energy

People who drain your energy seem to be part of life. It feels as though your blood is being drained right out of you. At times you do not even notice this straightaway. You simply begin noticing you no longer feel the way you did five minutes ago. Enter the energy vampire.

Frequently energy vampires are negative people. Negative people seem to have a need to find more negativity. If you are in a good mood, they start draining you, unaware of what they are doing.

A negative person will show any number of these traits: constant complaining, not being able to take responsibility for their actions, refusing to see the consequences of their choices, argumentative, histrionic behavior, attention seeking, seeing the glass as always half empty, etc.

Sometimes energy vampire behavior is related to the person's huge ego needing constant stroking and attention. You can also think of them as "drama queens" always needing to bring the focus back to them. While they are getting the attention, you feel tired, unhappy, drained, and exhausted. You might even find yourself getting a headache.

If you are in a situation where you cannot avoid people who drain you (for example, a family member or a coworker), this is the time to set boundaries. Think of it as setting a boundary to their behavior. This allows people to know where you stand. By doing so you are showing yourself respect. You are entitled to your own thoughts, opinions, and feelings, as are others.

In these circumstances, examples of boundaries you can set are:

- Set a physical boundary by stepping back and creating more space between you and the other person. You can visualize a "No Trespassing" sign. This alone will offer you a sense of power, if only for a moment.
- Make sure your behavior matches your words. Remember – actions speak louder than words.
- Communicate clearly, firmly, respectfully, and calmly in as few words as possible. If this is not possible in that moment, consider readdressing in a more appropriate time.

Thoughts to help you deal with the situation:

- Most importantly, learn to recognize what is going on when you start feeling drained. Ask yourself if it is the situation, conversation, or in fact, the behavior of the person whose company you are in.
- When you are in the company of an energy vampire, know it is reasonable to set a boundary and walk away.
- Realize this is a way of showing yourself respect.
- Excuse yourself politely even if you have to say it is to use the bathroom.
- Once you have walked away, gather your thoughts, assess the situation, and consider what are your possible options.
- If you cannot walk away, find a way to shield yourself, your energy from being drained any further. Try taking one step back, i.e., separate yourself physically if only a tiny bit, or focus on your breathing for a few seconds and exhale their energy.

A very wise friend told me once, "Remember, you can walk out of the room, but they are still in the room with themselves."

SETTING BOUNDARIES

Boundaries are guidelines, rules, or limits you have a right to create for yourself. With boundaries you are establishing what is acceptable to you. This offers others clarity on where you stand and how to behave with you and around you.

Healthy boundaries offer you:
- Self-respect and enhanced self-esteem
- Protection for your physical and emotional space
- Ways to maintain your personal power
- Strength, in that you are clear and confident about what does and does not work for you.
- A life aligned with your Core Values

If you say no, what are you saying yes to?

The answer is: to you.
You are choosing yourself as the priority – that is the bottom line of learning how to set a boundary. A boundary is set in order to stop yourself from being subjected to a certain type of behavior. It might suit the other person to behave in this manner, but it does not have to suit you to be in the environment.

Learning how to set boundaries helps you with energy vampires and others showing you no respect. These can be:
- Attention seeking, which could be based on an ego that needs endlessly to be seen and heard, i.e., high-maintenance people.
- It could be that to the person any attention is better than no attention. In this case, negative energy is being used to draw people in, to create a drama, to make a mountain out of a molehill – anything to keep the focus on themselves.
- Maybe the person feels alone and insecure.

Some sample situations where it is good to set a boundary:
- A friend always texts or calls you at work. You communicate that you cannot take calls and ask for this to be respected. Or you can stop answering altogether.
- A friend or colleague at work endlessly complains about the same problem over and over. This type of monologue leads nowhere, the problem stays. You do not have to keep listening! Tell him or her you no longer wish to hear about the problem but would be happy to help find a solution.
- Someone keeps criticizing or insulting you – how about communicating you do not appreciate being spoken to in that manner and you will no longer accept it. Walk out of the room if necessary. Communicate your boundary – make it known and learn to be consistent with your behavior. Do not forget "actions speak louder than words."

If setting a boundary relates to your work environment, saying no to your boss might be the wrong choice. Ask yourself what else could you say no to in order to accommodate your boss's request.

These are the most common reasons people say yes when in fact no might serve better:
- Finding it hard not to help
- Fearful of seeming bad mannered
- Fear of losing out
- Fear of being difficult
- Fear of not being reliable
- Fear of hurting someone's feelings

Ask the following questions for motivation to make this switch in your behavior:

- What can I gain from saying no?

  For example, saying no to an offer to go out because what you really need is time at home for yourself. By saying no, you are giving yourself that time.

- How about saying not now, if this is not the right time, or situation, for you to say no?

Find a situation where you will feel the least resistance to start practicing this. I started by saying, "I will get back to you and let you know if and when I can." This way I bought myself some time to consider exactly how important the person and/or request was and what I could lose or gain by saying either no or not now.

Communicate, firmly and calmly, what the boundary is you are setting. Not only will this help you, the other person will have a better understanding of what is going on.

Allow yourself time and patience to make this change and remember always to give yourself a pat on the back when you made yourself the priority.

It is important to handle this change with good manners, grace, and respect. Learning to set a boundary does not mean you can be rude and disrespectful.

It can be a difficult new habit to learn. You might find yourself feeling guilty so be sure to take care of yourself. In moments like these remind yourself you are learning how to take better care of yourself.

Do not be surprised if people start treating you with more respect.

SELF-SABOTAGE

This is a big topic and unique to each person, depending on what exactly your self-sabotage routine is and how it shows up. Have you ever wondered just how much you hold yourself back and/or limit yourself with self-sabotaging behavior patterns?

Self-sabotage can be described as running interference on yourself. I suggest awareness is the first and most important step toward dealing with it – the awareness of this pattern's existence. Everybody has an inner saboteur; the inner critic. Think of the times when you have asked yourself, "Why did I do that?" I like to think of self-sabotage as a virus in the software. The job is to get rid of it and run a new program. Healthy routines are those that move your life forward, such as maintaining some kind of equilibrium, maintaining your physical and mental health.

A routine becomes sabotage when it keeps you stuck in the same place, treading water, not moving forward. What started these self-sabotage routines and where they come from is well researched in psychology.

There are countless bad habits and routines but the most common are:
- Procrastination
- Negative self-feedback or mind chatter
- Self-medication with drugs, alcohol, or food – you might enjoy the momentary pleasure but in truth you are giving your power over to a routine that is not healthy
- Keeping your schedule full, while neglecting or not scheduling valuable downtime.

Focus on recognizing and accepting the self-sabotage routines you may have and how they affect your behavior and the quality of your daily life. At this point I suggest there is no need to figure out where the inner saboteur comes from. Instead, I suggest observing yourself and becoming aware of the routines you have in place that keep you going around in circles.

Shedding self-sabotage is about no longer being your own worst enemy.

Observe yourself and become aware of what and how you handle and react to certain situations – raise your awareness to your behavior. You can make mental notes or an actual list of your observations.

The next step is to find a new program to run. You can do this with the help and support of a professional coach. For the moment, the best first step is recognizing a self-sabotaging pattern when it is in action, or after it happened.

NEEDINESS IN A RELATIONSHIP

Many people can relate to being in a relationship and feeling needy; some even think that they are nothing without a partner. This might also be a version of codependency. Thinking you are nothing without a partner is based on believing you are incomplete, or not whole on our own. The sad news is that more often than not, neediness can be a relationship killer.

Getting beyond this neediness means having the desire to grow and become true to yourself. This involves getting to know who you are at a deeper level, in a sense, connecting with yourself. With this, your capacity to love becomes more unconditional. You no longer need, or indeed want, your partner to need you. You start seeing/feeling yourself as a more whole and complete person. One of the consequences of this is that you wish the same of, and for, your loved one. Love, true love, love from the heart is all about loving the person unconditionally.

Life transforms itself when neediness disappears. When you take responsibility for your life – start taking responsibility for your choices, and most importantly the consequences of those choices – you start feeling this transformation. For example, if you choose to think you are nothing without your partner, a consequence of that is that you continue to behave and act as if you are nothing without him or her. You are giving your own personal power away to your partner in this case.

Neediness is an emotion created by fear. This fear can create child-like behavior: being demanding and unreasonable, feeling insecure, with resultant jealousy, obsessiveness, anger, wanting to control, etc. On the path of personal growth you gain confidence by connecting to the part of you that is strong and secure. With this growth the entire nature of the relationship has a chance to change. It is then that real, unconditional love is possible.

If you find neediness is a large part of your relationship, consider making some changes. These questions might be useful to ask yourself. Best to have pen and paper handy and make some lists or notes.

1. What exactly do I think I cannot do without him or her?
2. What exactly do I think I cannot be without him or her?
3. How do I feel when I am in my partner's company?
4. How does my partner make me feel about myself?
5. If I felt better about myself, what would be different? How would I feel?
6. What would I change?
7. Who could support me in making this change?
8. How would I proceed to get started?
9. What might hold me back from doing this?

This topic is multilayered and is best approached with a professional. The end result of moving beyond your fears and getting rid of the neediness will make you more loving, and your partner will, in turn, become more loving as well. It will take time and dedication but will prove to be worth every minute you invest in yourself and every step you take.

JUST THINK POSITIVE – WHY THOSE THREE WORDS MAKE ME CRAZY!

The reason I feel this way is, in my opinion in order to think positive, a positive mind-set is necessary. Naturally even positive thinkers can have moments of drifting off into negative thoughts. Their strength is to return to a more positive approach rather than go to the place of doom and gloom of a negative thinker.

To *just think positive* it is necessary to have a positive mind-set.

When you are struggling to stay positive about something, you are probably feeling stressed. This might be the result of feeling uncertain or lacking clarity about the situation, person or project, or any number of other reasons. So when I hear that the advice given by a helpful, supportive friend or colleague is to just think positive, I am so tempted to ask: "And *exactly* how do you suggest your friend or colleague does this while feeling stressed?"

Of course changing your mind-set or perspective from negative to positive is brilliant advice. It is the expectation that this happens in a flash that makes me crazy. It is not as if you can flick a switch in your mind.

Based on research in the field of neuroscience, stress activates a stress response in the body. One of these responses is that cognitive resources, such as focus and clear rational thinking, are depleted. It is a fact that when emotions of stress kick in, cognitive resources are first to be disrupted. Emotions overpower thinking in that moment. Without creating a safer, calmer environment, your thinking will stay limited.

Switch to feeling and being able to think more positively by initially breaking the energy of that very moment.

The fastest way to take charge of stress, i.e., negative thoughts, is by involving your senses: take a walk, listen to music, be creative, cook something, bake a cake... do anything that you find soothing that will distract you from your thoughts right now. As my mother always told us, "Busy hands are happy hands." If you are at work, allow yourself a short break away from your desk, take a couple of deep breaths, and interrupt the energy of your mood in that moment. You can always get something to drink, have a bathroom break or any other short break away you can consider appropriate. Then return to the situation and take another look at it.

This rule applies to life at work, as well as your personal life.

Helpful guidance tips on the type of question you can ask yourself to feel more positive:
- What is good about the situation/my life/this person/the project?
- What actually is working/good about this, i.e., what is positive?
- Once you are aware of these points, move on to:
- What exactly is making me feel negative? Be specific with your answers.

Here are some ideas:
- This situation lacks clarity or does not agree with my values
- It is the lack of direction in my life
- The way this person speaks to me is insulting
- This project is badly managed

What might I be assuming?

Here are some ideas:
- I am assuming that I will not find clarity
- I am assuming I do not know how to find the answers
- I am assuming that I will not be able to ask them to show some respect

- I am assuming I cannot influence how this project is managed
- How can you influence those thoughts or the situation? How else can you look at this?
- Never underestimate how talking about it out loud can help, so...
- Who can be supportive right now? Who could I talk to?
- When you feel you are thinking clearly again, explore what can be influenced *now in this very moment*
- If there is an action you can take, follow through with that.

Sometimes accepting that you cannot do anything to change the situation is the most helpful step. To me this falls under the heading "You cannot change people, but you can change how you react." In other words *acceptance* is the most empowering step you can take right now.

This is a skill, a life skill, well worth acquiring. It will help you feel stronger, more secure, and raise your self-esteem. Practice this approach over and over; soon you will know that you are thinking more positively because you know you can turn things around.

Daily Habits

THOUGHTS KEEPING YOU AWAKE AT NIGHT?

Finding it difficult to sleep? Whichever thoughts are keeping you awake clearly want some attention. Otherwise they would not still be lurking around in the back of your head, keeping your mind and body from unwinding and relaxing into a good night's sleep. Ideally, sleep helps process our emotions. I look at a good night's sleep as comparable to an effective filing system – while sleeping, your mind files what needs to be kept and your emotions discard anything unnecessary. Your emotions then have time to settle, and your intuition has a chance to speak to you. A good night's sleep allows for a fresh mind, the possibility of a new approach, to start the day feeling more balanced.

Thinking habits and problem-solving skills, no matter how good and effective they are, do not always allow for the mind to be at peace every night. There is only so much we can do with our mind. Being anxious is not a medical condition; it comes from the mind. Anxiety comes when thoughts are running away with you. These thoughts, more often than not, are from the immediate past or about the future – relating to something that may or may not happen tomorrow. The best way to shift your thoughts away from worries is to focus on something else.

One proven method is to pay close attention to your breathing. Try this method:

- Take a couple of breaths, first into your heart then down into your belly, even down to your toes, and then exhale through your entire body. Do this with emotion if you feel like it. Repeat this as many times as feels right. Then slowly begin to inhale in a more focused manner, down into your belly, and exhale, feeling the breath leave you again. Notice a calmness coming over you. Your mind might still be throwing the disturbing thoughts at you, but just acknowledge this and return your focus to your breathing. Keep repeating this for several minutes if possible.

- When you are calmer, begin to focus on what is bothering you. Perhaps you are uncomfortable with an upcoming conversation or are wondering if you could have/should have handled a situation better/differently. Perhaps it is a situation about which you feel helpless. Whatever it is, give it some attention.

- Attempt to narrow it down to have clarity on exactly what is keeping you awake. Break the problem down into sections. Imagine placing the various sections into different boxes and label the boxes. Breaking down the issue will offer some clarity and make the problem more manageable. In the morning you can start considering what action-oriented steps need to be taken.

- Depending on the situation, a good question to ask yourself might be: What action, if any, might I be able to take right now in the middle of the night that could help resolve this?

- If nothing comes to mind, accept that you are not avoiding dealing with the problem, but you are merely asking it to go away until you are rested and more capable of handling it.

- Knowing you will be dealing with the issue in the morning, take more deep breaths and with each exhalation let some of the feelings attached to the thoughts dissipate. Visualize putting the problem into a boat and pushing the boat out to sea or placing it onto a cloud that drifts away over your head. Maybe one of the sheep you are counting that jump over the fence could take this problem with him. Use an image that feels right to you so that this problem goes away for a couple of hours. Continue to breathe deeply while doing this.

This is about being realistic as to what can and cannot be done in the moment. Worrying about something you can do nothing about in that moment will only make the problem seem bigger. Allow yourself to be realistic about what can and cannot be achieved by resting rather than worrying. And get a good night's sleep.

Having a bad day?

In reality there is no such thing as a bad day. If you interpret or perceive something to be bad, then that is the way it is. Things happen that make some days harder than others, this is true for everyone. It is how you approach it that makes the difference. I like the quote: What is the difference between a weed and a flower? Answer: An opinion. If you judge or perceive something to be bad, that is exactly what it is to you.

Being in a bad mood happens to everybody, but it is what you do about it that changes the outcome of the day.

Telling yourself to cheer up or pretending all is well when you are feeling that way rarely helps.

It is best not to fight it. Go with your feelings and let them out. If you are angry, do some anger management. If you are frustrated, lack clarity, or are overwhelmed, figure out what you can influence in that moment. What exactly can you do to help you feel less frustrated, or what can you do to figure out ways to unclear or reduce the feeling of being overwhelmed? For example, if you are tired, make sure you find some downtime even if it means going to bed at 8 p.m. There is always something you can influence in each moment.

Some thoughts to consider when you are having a bad day:

- Acknowledge your bad mood in order for you to be able to do something about it.
- Ask yourself what specifically is making this a bad day.
- What would make it better?
- If you had any influence, how could you make a difference?
- What are the chances of you being able to do something to make it better?
- How could you help yourself? If you cannot come up with something, then ask yourself what advice would you give to a friend?

- Think of a couple of actions you could take.
- Choose the one that feels right.
- What do you have to do now to make that happen?
- And after that...
- You can influence how you see or cope with the day.

As harsh as it sounds, it is true that if you are not part of the solution, you are part of the problem. There is always something that can be done, no matter how small.

Take a difficult day hour by hour if necessary, but handle it.

GET ORGANIZED

Whether you are working full-time, part-time, or not at all, it can sometimes seem impossible to juggle all the daily requirements and be organized.

For motivation:

- Imagine what it will be like once you are more organized.
- Imagine how you will feel when you have managed to make the necessary changes to how you presently plan your days.
- If you lack time, ask yourself: What will it be like to no longer feel like I do not have enough time? For example, you might think that having enough time will give you a sense of calm, a sense of good management, your sense of humor back, or a sense of power in that you have been able to take charge of this problem and influence it.
- How will it be to have some time for myself, get more done?
- You might find yourself thinking you will be a happier, better parent, healthier, more energetic, more creative, and more inspired.
- Remind yourself of these thoughts to keep your motivation going until you are better at planning and being organized.

Once you are motivated, ask yourself the following questions.

Have paper and a pen handy to take notes, make lists, or get creative.

- Explore what you can change in your daily routine.
- Consider specifically what has to change.
- How realistic are your expectations that you will be able to follow through?

- Perhaps your expectations are too high because the day only has twenty-four hours, or you are not allowing yourself to have low-energy days.
- Perhaps you need to ask for some outside help.
- Perhaps you need to say no to something for the moment. Until the new plan can start making a difference, create time by saying no to something in the past you have said yes to without thinking.

Having identified what has to change, consider the actions you now will take:

- Take one step at a time, slowly allowing yourself to get used to the changes this will create.
- Consider if it is really necessary to do everything on your list today. Some of the items could be moved to tomorrow and the world would still go around!
- When the time is right, take the next step.

Remember to give yourself some credit for your choice to start making some changes. Giving yourself a pat on the back, no matter how small you think this step is, will keep you positive, motivated, and able to appreciate the results.

Bear in mind that as with all changes, you will probably slip up, but then remember that tomorrow is a new day and you can start getting organized afresh.

HOW TO VISUALIZE SOMETHING

Visualizing is using your imagination to see something in your mind's eye. Imagination is key to life: it is helpful to successfully move away from any negative thoughts and feelings. There are numerous tools and techniques to support getting the most out of life. Visualization is one of these tools. Use it to see the successful you, yourself as you wish to be. This is a powerful tool practiced by many athletes, businesspeople, and others from all walks of life.

The action of picturing yourself as relaxed and confident, as successful or already having achieved a certain goal, stimulates your body with endorphins and naturally starts building up confidence and courage. You and your problems slowly drift farther apart when you visualize how you wish to be. In life, when you focus on failure you are in fact letting yourself down by not truly believing in your potential.

Different ways to regard visualizations are:
    1. Those that support you in creating what you want.
    2. Those that abolish what you no longer want.
    3. Those that confirm your successes.

To experience how easy visualization can be, let's use the example of going to a place of calm. Always begin with breathing exercises.
- Sit comfortably and take a couple of breaths with your eyes shut. Breathe in deeply through your nose and out through your mouth.
- Maintain the focus on your breathing, feeling the air go in and out of your body.
- Relax... allow yourself to take time... count backward from twenty before you go into a visualization.

- Select an image in your memory bank, perhaps of a place you love.
- Pretend you are there.
- Take a walk around, look at all the details, notice the smell, the feel of it.
- If your mind tries to pull you away, focus back on your breathing until you can bring the image up again... and the feeling of being there.
- This might take some practice. You will find that each time you sit and go to that special place, you will be able to stay there longer and longer, even if only for a few seconds respectively.
- Be patient with yourself.

Always allow yourself to appreciate the feeling of having been there, no matter how long it lasted. You did it!

I like to pick a new image for the day when I am out on my morning walk, or in the summer when I swim in the lake. I take a few seconds, or longer, to really take the image in and be able to hold it in my mind's eye. If necessary later in the day I can bring it up again if I need some energy or to distract myself.

Behavior Change

CHANGE YOUR REACTIVE BEHAVIOR

Learning how to respond to a situation rather than reacting to it brings huge rewards. Needless to say, it is one of those changes of behavior that is easier said than done. However, it can be achieved.

Responding rather than reacting means you will have taken time to consider the situation and which response and consequent outcome best suits you.

The difference between reacting and responding:

To *respond* means you are able to influence your emotions in the moment when something has triggered them. You are able to stop yourself from saying or doing something you might regret. You stop yourself long enough until your emotions have settled down and you can think clearly.

To *react* means you are not able to influence your emotions and you act full of emotion rather than from a place of clarity.

What you gain by stopping knee-jerk reactions is a sense of strength, achievement, power to influence, calmness, plus an increase in your self-esteem. The rewards will be felt not only in your private life, but also at work.

As with all behavioral changes time and patience will be necessary, and you should allow yourself to make mistakes during this reprogramming.

Different kinds of reactions:

- Damage can result from spontaneous reactions and sometimes cannot be undone, e.g., in situations where a good first impression is crucial. During a job interview, an overreaction or reacting without consideration can result in not getting called back for a second interview.

- There are also reactions that fall under the heading of the best defense is a good offense. If you get triggered, you might react defensively. The outcome of an offensive reaction is rarely what you would like it to be.
- Some people create situations in which they can react – the bigger, louder, and more dramatically, the better. These are people who thrive on chaos. This kind of dramatic reaction allows them to control the situation. In this case, it is best to walk away.
- During emergencies or a life-and-death situation, your instinctive reactions serve you well. These are not the reactions I am referring to here.

Everybody has certain relationships or situations that bring out the worst reactions or overreactions. Feeling busy and stressed can magnify a reaction. In contrast, when you are relaxed, you are better able to take time to assess the options and possible responses to achieve your desired result.

Eight tips to help you learn how to stop reacting and start responding:

1. Commit yourself to making this change in your behavior. Accept that it will take time and require some patience.
2. Start noticing what triggers you. Maybe it is a certain type of conversation, being with a particular person, being ignored, getting interrupted, feeling time pressure, or being unable to communicate clearly.
3. Get to know what specifically triggers a reaction in you. What is it about the tone of voice, the chosen words, the message, or body language that pushes that button in you?
4. Once you have familiarized yourself with the triggers, imagine how it would be or look if you dealt with them in a different manner than usual.

5. Imagine a situation in the future when you respond without immediately reacting. How will you feel? Who will you be?

6. Now think about what the possible options are in the moment when your trigger goes off. How can you buy yourself some time to avoid reacting? Is it possible to leave the room, ask the person to call you back later, take some deep breaths, find the self-respect to say, "I will get back to you on that"?

7. Get to know this feeling. It will encourage and motivate you.

8. Make a list, if only a mental one, of the steps you plan on taking to stop yourself from reacting.

In summary, by learning how to respond rather than react you are giving yourself:

- *Choice* – having taken the time to reflect upon the situation, you tend to have more options to choose from than just the one, which was a reaction.

- *Power* – you keep your personal power by taking the best possible care of yourself in not reacting, and waiting until you can respond constructively. This makes you feel strong.

- *Less Stress* – by buying some time to make a constructive choice you avoid the emotions in a reaction that drain you.

- *Calm* – knowing that you can cope with situations that in the past have pushed your buttons brings a calm, an inner peace into your life.

- *Increased Self-Esteem* – another step up the ladder with this added new tool in your personal growth and development automatically increases your self-esteem.

A REQUEST DOES NOT SIT RIGHT — WHAT TO DO

This situation can arise in all sorts of ways on various emotional levels. It could be a simple request by a friend, colleague, or boss, or could concern a more emotional issue within a relationship. If your gut feeling, that inner voice, lets you know there is an issue in this request making you uncomfortable, the best approach is to allow yourself to gather more information before you make a decision. Feeling uncomfortable and following through to please someone else more often than not means you are choosing not to please yourself. In other words, you are putting more value onto them and, in the process, giving your power away.

Helpful guidance questions to ask yourself:
1. Gather more information about this request – get clarity.
2. Once you understand more clearly what is driving their request, you can proceed, if you so choose. However...
3. If you are still uncomfortable, ask yourself if you might be compromising your values. This is what could be making you feel uncomfortable.
4. If you feel your values are being compromised, realize that you have the right to choose not to comply with this request.
5. Proceed to explain your reasons for not wishing to comply.
6. By doing this you are showing both parties the deserved respect.

Consider this excerpt **Personal Bill of Rights** from "Healing the Child Within" (1987) by Charles L. Whitfield, M.D., when you next find yourself in a situation where you are asked to do something and it does not feel right:

- I have numerous choices in my life beyond mere survival.
- I have a right to follow my own values and standards.
- I have a right to recognize and accept my own value system.
- I have a right to say no to anything when I feel I am not ready, it is unsafe, or violates my values.
- I have a right to dignity and respect.
- I have a right to make my own decisions.
- I have the right to determine and honor my own priorities.
- I have the right not to be responsible for others' behavior, actions, feelings, or problems.
- I have a right to make mistakes and not be perfect.
- I have a right to all my feelings.
- I have a right to be angry with someone I love.
- I have a right to feel scared and to say, "I'm afraid."
- I have a right to my own personal space and time needs.
- I have a right to change and grow.

TAKE RESPONSIBILITY FOR YOUR ACTIONS

Every decision has a consequence.

First comes a decision followed by an action resulting in a consequence. Having the strength to take responsibility for your actions, even if the consequences are not exactly what you planned or had hoped for, shows personal power. This comes from the ability to stand by yourself. When results do not work out as expected, a natural tendency can be to find someone or something else to blame. The blame game avoids responsibility. It is not always easy feeling blame for something that went wrong. Yet, there is a price to pay. As harsh as it sounds, making excuses or blaming others for a negative outcome is often seen in those who fail. This can relate to life or career, health, or happiness in general.

The following are questions that can help when you are finding it difficult to take responsibility:

- What did I do, or did I not do, to help create this situation I now find myself in?
- What can I learn from what just happened?
- How could I have handled this better?
- What was I hoping to achieve? What specific result was I looking for?
- If I was trying to blame someone else, then what was I trying to avoid by attempting to blame them?
- Imagine how it would be if I changed this behavior.
- What will I gain if I change my behavior?
- What, if anything, will I lose if I change this behavior?
- What can I start doing differently to be able to start taking responsibility?
- Write down your thoughts and refer back to them.

Owning your choices and maintaining your power is part of standing on your own. In accepting responsibility you are showing a willingness to develop your character. The stronger your character, the better your life will become. Accepting total responsibility for the consequences of your decisions and actions will give you strength by making you feel good about yourself. Finding solutions takes place with greater ease when you are feeling good about yourself.

Social Skills

THE ELEPHANT IN THE ROOM — WHAT MAKES YOU AVOID CERTAIN TOPICS OF CONVERSATION?

Addressing the issue would bring clarity and awareness. And yet it is fascinating how quickly talking about a topic that in fact is hurting everybody in some way or another is avoided. The problem could be dealt with and a sense of clarity, peace, and calm could return. Yet the elephant, the sometimes very large elephant, is ignored and walked around; the behavior is to pretend the elephant does not actually exist.

Imagine you are in a situation with an elephant in the room. For example, let us say the issue is a miscommunication:

It is painfully obvious you are walking around the elephant. The air is so thick you could cut it, anybody entering the room can feel the bad energy, it is that obvious. Rather than asking what the reasons for this behavior are, you mask your hurt, confusion, frustration, or anger by being superficial and polite. If someone asks you what is wrong or if you're okay, you answer: "Nothing" or "I am fine."

Think about it, your polite "I am fine" in response is in fact a miscommunication. You are doing exactly what hurt, confused, frustrated, or made you angry... not communicating openly. You are withholding the truth by not communicating it. Communicating more openly would be to say one of the following statements:

- You did not tell me you were going to ...
- I need more clarity on how to ...
- I seem to have misunderstood ...
- You hurt my feelings by ...
- I feel disrespected when you ...

From my coaching clients I hear more and more examples of the same scenario being true in the workplace. Employees are fearful of asking their managers or leaders for more clarity relating to the objectives or processes of a project. Bosses believe it is a waste to spend time, interact, and work more closely with their team. Often the reason being that the work will fall behind!

The stories go on and on. There are lots of elephants out there!

Being the one who opens up the conversation can create apprehension. It can feel like walking into unknown territory. From my own experience, both personal and professional, one possible reason behind this tends to be some kind of fear of. In this case it could be a fear of the truth. You were not told because the other person thought you would not approve or that you might be judgmental. They might be worried that telling you what the problem is could result in creating a problem that is unresolvable. Or, they simply might be worried about losing you.

Being the first one to bring the elephant out into the open will only ever give you strength. Having courage to take a step always brings strength with it.

Ask yourself any of the following questions if you find yourself in a room with an elephant:

- What will happen if I do nothing? (If everything stays the same, I remain in this place of feeling drained by the situation on some level and it continues to waste good energy and time.)
- What will happen if I do something? (The situation can actually change by your knowing what specifically needs to be cleared up, moved on from, healed.)
- What is the worst that could happen if I bring the elephant out into the open? (I lose the friendship, feel judged or misunderstood.)
- How will it make me feel about myself to take this action? (Proud, stronger, efficient, openhearted to myself and the other person.)

- What will I gain? (Self-respect, clarity, more energy, being more true to my values and myself.)
- How do I best plan the time and space to address this issue? Being realistic is very important at this moment. The timing for bringing the elephant out into the open is best planned for when it suits both parties, when there is enough time, space, and a good environment. So choose the time with respect for both parties.

There will always be situations with elephants in the room. How long you ignore them is up to you. How long you make the choice to feel bad rather than confront the truth is up to you, as Susan Jeffers' book title suggests, *Feel the Fear... and Do It Anyway.* On a personal level, you can only gain from being the one who has the strength to clear things up. Whatever you feel you might be losing is most probably better off lost, if indeed you do lose it. More often than not, talking about the issue brings clarity and a resolution.

IMPROVE YOUR CONVERSATION SKILLS

Good rapport is one of the elements that creates a harmonious environment for successful communication. A satisfying, balanced conversation means the parties involved feel comfortable, relaxed, calm, and safe.

Points to remember that create a feeling of good rapport:

Body Language:

Actions speak louder than words.

Our body language, with its nonverbal communication, forms 55% of our message. No matter how hard we might try to be nonjudgmental, we do start reading someone when they walk in the room. We look at their physical appearance, how they are dressed and groomed. We look for things with which we can identify.

To create the feeling of being at ease, you can stand like them, walk like them, sit like them, use the same gestures, match their eye contact, even breathe in tune with them. This is called matching or mirroring. Matching is doing exactly what they do. For example, if they are leaning forward, giving the feeling of being interested, you can also very subtly lean forward. Mirroring is duplicating with the mirror image of their behavior.

All of this should never be done in an exaggerated manner. You do not intend to mock them or show them disrespect. Your aim is to make them comfortable in your presence. Mirroring someone's facial expression is a good practice, for example smiling if they smile.

If you are interested in a conversation, your body will reveal this by the way it is acting. You will be relaxed, hold eye contact, and concentrate on what is being said.

Quality of Voice:

How we use our voice represents 38% of the impact in our conversation. It is not what we say, it is how it is said. Adapting to each other's volume, tone, and pitch can make an enormous difference on the impact and meaning of what we say.

Choice of Words:

If 55% of our communication is through our body language and 38% is the use of our voice, that leaves only 7% for the words we choose. A wrong word can stifle conversation. For example, if you say, "Why did you do that?" the reaction would be one of defense. If you instead say, "What motivated you to do that?" this gives space for thought and self-reflection.

Creating a feeling of natural rapport can be compared to dancing with a partner, where one leads and the other follows. You are cooperating with each other, not competing. If you are leading and your partner has picked up your lead, you know you are on your way to establishing a good relationship based on mutual respect and natural rapport.

By applying these skills you will be creating a harmonious environment. The result of natural rapport is good and effective communication. This allows conversations to have better results and makes it easier to approach difficult subjects.

BEING COMFORTABLE AROUND STRANGERS

Even if you have done it a hundred times, the thought of walking into a room full of strangers can be daunting. It is perfectly natural to feel nervous when facing a new situation – most people do. Regardless of whether you are introverted or extroverted, everybody can remember feeling uneasy at some point in their life when having to walk into a room full of strangers.

It helps to remind yourself that chances are there will be another person, if not many, who are feeling the same as you are. With that thought in mind, take a slow stroll around the room and find someone standing alone, go up to that person and introduce yourself. I find opening the conversation by offering my business card is a great way to break the ice. With this gesture it allows the person to take a moment to read it and have something to comment on. There is a very good chance that your courage for walking up to them will be rewarded with a sigh of relief and a smile, especially if they have been standing alone. A lovely Burmese saying is: "If you see someone without a smile, give them yours." Smiling works wonders to break uncomfortable moments.

The classic networking tools come in handy:
- Focus on the other people and what they have to say.
- Show interest in them and encourage them to talk about themselves. Everybody loves to talk about themselves... their holiday, their children, etc.
- Use the rapport building tools – match their body language and speak in the same tone of voice. This will put them at ease.
- Helpful suggestions for the moments just before you walk into the room. These are useful to practice while you are getting ready as well.

- Acknowledge you are feeling nervous and lacking confidence in this moment.
- Imagine what it feels like to have confidence. How would you like that to feel? It can help to think of someone you know who has confidence and picture what it would be like to be that person. Or pretend you have a pair of confidence shoes on that give you support and make you strong when you wear them.
- Picture yourself as a confident person.
- What does it feel like? Take a couple of deep breaths and with each inhalation feel that confidence.
- Acknowledge that you now have the choice to step into those shoes. It helps if you visualize yourself putting on an actual pair of shoes. Remember these are your confidence shoes!
- Step into those shoes, take a deep breath, and walk into that room. Your aim is to go and help the other person standing there all alone who is not wearing their confidence shoes!
- Be pleased with yourself.

Self-Management

CLEAR YOUR HEAD FROM MIND CHATTER

Don't Believe Everything You Think was on a bumper sticker I came across some years ago during one of my morning walks. I had probably walked past this bumper sticker one hundred times, but this time the words spoke to me. Why? I was ready to hear them and take some action. It also amuses me that bumper stickers are rarely seen on cars in the area of Switzerland I live in. In my mind this made seeing this particular one all the more of a sign. It was my time to learn how to deal with mind chatter!

My reality that morning was: I was walking alongside a beautiful lake, the sun was about to rise, and it was early enough to not yet have the song of the birds overpowered by the sounds of traffic and early morning life. So what was I doing miles away from this peaceful situation, lost in my mind chatter full of negative thoughts? I had lost the morning to these thoughts; I believed what I was thinking was true. While I was walking on this lovely morning, I realized that these were merely thoughts... they were only my projections, which had nothing to do with my morning walk. I realized that I was treating these thoughts as if they were the reality of that moment, when, in fact, I was out walking, surrounded by beauty, and not in the negative place where my mind was!

I am a big believer in breaking the energy of that very moment when your thoughts are bouncing you off all walls like a ping-pong ball.

These steps are helpful when you need to clear your head:
- Take a deep breath in through your nose and exhale through your mouth. Do this at least three times. You will see that bringing your focus to your breath is already stopping the other thoughts from bombarding you.

- Before the negative thoughts get a chance to return (and they will try their hardest to do so!), bring your attention to the present moment. By this I mean: look at the room you are in, look out the window if possible – focus on nature if you see it. Do whatever possible to keep the focus on something in your immediate surroundings. If you have access to nature let it share some of its powerful energy with you – look at the sky, admire the little plant growing in the middle of train tracks or out of a sidewalk.

- Check in and see if you have managed to break the string of thoughts. If not, keep focusing on your surroundings or your breath.

Your mind will start settling down. Once this happens you will be able to start thinking more clearly. This is the time to consider what you can do and how you can influence the issue that was going round and round in your head as mind chatter.

Remember these steps for the future moments when you need some space in your head, and be present.

Do Not Believe Everything You Think. Believing what you think has the tendency to throw you into the space/place that you are not actually in. You end up in a projected reality, not the truth of the moment.

BREAK YOUR ACTION PLAN INTO SMALLER REALISTIC STEPS

The magic of small steps can help you achieve remarkable results. Today's lifestyle does not allow much free time. Bear this in mind: small steps are more realistic, more achievable, and keep your day-to-day life feeling more balanced.

Consider these tips:

1. For motivation consider what will be different once you have completed the action plan. Really take some time to think about this. You will be able to draw on these thoughts if you are lacking focus and motivation along the way.

2. Write down all the detailed steps necessary to complete the plan. What changes have to be considered and made? Make a list. As the ideas come to you, write them down. At this point do not pay attention to the order of priority, just write.

3. Rewrite the list in order of priority. What exactly has to be done first? What follows?

4. Consider whether taking the steps in this order is realistic. Do you have enough time? Do you need support? If yes, whose support do you need? Do they have time?

5. If anything has been left out, add it.

6. Adjust your steps if necessary along the way. Stay open to calibrating your targets and steps if necessary. It is perfectly okay to revisit and revise them to ease the load along the way. It is much wiser to keep things realistic than to be tense and under pressure. Most importantly, make sure these targets and steps are aligned with your personality.

7. Take the first step, then the next, and so on... one at a time.

8. Appreciate yourself for having worked this out.

9. Well done! Do not forget to celebrate the small gains along the way.

Do things in the style that suits you. Remember, life changes constantly and therefore requires you to go with the flow when something needs adjusting or adapting. You are more likely to reach the goal when you do what works for you.

How I create a mind map to help me with actionable steps:

I draw a circle in the middle of a big piece of paper. In the circle I write down the goal. Then like rays of sunshine coming out of the circle, I write down the steps necessary to take one by one to reach the goal.

To use a very simple example: if my goal is to schedule some free time, I will draw a smiley face in the middle as that represents me with more free time!

1. Then the first step (ray of sunshine) will be to examine my calendar for the next month.

2. Block out two-hour time frames on at least two days per working week.

3. Write down what I want to do with this free time (walks, creativity, sleep, cooking, doing nothing at all, etc.)

4. I include obstacles that could get in the way of these time slots so I am aware of anything unexpected.

In the end I have a piece of paper that looks like a sun with the various steps to take. Obviously this is a most basic example. I use this technique also for more complicated projects to help me have an oversight. I find it really supports me with time management as I can see with clarity what the workload involves.

STOP BEATING YOURSELF UP

Most people seem to have the habit of beating themselves up. You might criticize yourself for something you said, did, or did not do or say. Being critical and disappointed with your behavior is not productive in any way. If anything, it drains your personal power and consequently makes you less productive on all levels. Luckily, however, it is one that can be recognized for what it is and slowly changed.

Some of the realities around this habit to consider:
- It robs you of lots of good quality energy
- It wastes your time
- It is harmful
- It throws you off balance
- It will keep you from being the best version of yourself

How this habit started, developed, and grew into being part of your behavior patterns could be due to any number of reasons, dating back to earlier days or more recent occurrences in your life. Everyone has an inner voice that loves to shout negative, disempowering thoughts when given the opportunity. Learning how not to listen to the negativity is the challenge. The goal is to replace the negative thoughts with positive feelings and statements about yourself. The motivation to appreciate all the good you have and all you have to offer instead of keeping the focus on the weaker parts, will help you learn how to stop beating yourself up. This is, admittedly, easier said than done, and it takes time, patience, and practice.

Whatever you are beating yourself up about, understand that you can find a different way to react. Maybe something went wrong or you are disappointed because you have not taken care of yourself. Did you miss an opportunity, fail to reach a goal, handle a conversation badly, or feel you have let someone down? When your habit is to beat yourself up you will find countless reasons to do so.

Whatever the story of the moment is, if you want to help yourself out of this feeling and stop the beating, take some time to settle down (put the stick down), and explore the situation.

These tips will guide you to stop:

1. Ask yourself what triggered this. Did you do something or did you say something you wish you hadn't done? Was it someone's behavior that pushed one of your buttons? Try to achieve a clear understanding of what has started this behavior now.

2. Think about what exactly you are criticizing yourself for. This could be difficult to narrow down so take the time to think carefully about it. If it was something someone said to you, ask yourself what exactly he or she said and what might he or she have been hoping to gain with their comment? Maybe you felt criticized by their suggestion and this pushed your "I need everybody's approval" button?

3. Whatever you understand the issue to be, acknowledge and realize you have chosen to beat yourself up over this. This was a choice you made even if not consciously.

4. Having recognized you are beating yourself up, you now wish to make a different choice: not to put yourself down anymore but find a way to feel better!

5. There is no need to intellectualize and rationalize it all. The point is to stop the beating, get your power back, and get back into balance instead of wasting more time with this behavior.

6. To help regain your balance, focus briefly on some of the points you feel good about. Think of all your good qualities, friends, family, achievements, etc. These thoughts will support a better mind-set.

7. Now, take some proactive steps to break out of the mood. Listen to some music, call a friend, take a walk around the block, make a cup of tea – anything to help turn off the negative voice.

8. Whenever the voice tries to creep back in, take charge and tell it: "Not now."

9. If you cannot manage to truly break away from the feeling left over from the beating, get some rest and start afresh tomorrow. Sometimes the only action that really helps is some sleep, during which time your natural filing system can bring back some balance, and your body will get the necessary recharging to start a new day with a fresh attitude.

It is realistic to be negative at times. Accept this calmly rather than forcing yourself to be ideologically positive. Know that there is always something you can do when a mood gets you down, if only an action that will distract your attention momentarily. Take a walk or a bath, or do anything creative, like draw.

OBSESSING OVER NEGATIVE THOUGHTS

You choose what you will wear and eat, what films you see, who you socialize with, etc. You make choices all day long in your professional and personal life. In the same way, you also have the choice of which thoughts to focus on. The nice, happy thoughts, of course, are not a problem for they give energy, put a smile on your face, and are inspiring as well as motivating.

Everybody has negative thoughts. They are the ones that are easy to obsess over and rob you of energy, leaving you feeling drained. Believe it or not, how long you allow negative thoughts to influence your mood, day, or even life is up to you. Every thought you have either weakens you or strengthens you.

It is important to realize that thoughts are not reality. Assumptions are good examples of this. Just because you assume something does not make it true.

When you are struggling to stop obsessing about something, remind yourself that you have a choice to move on to a thought that might make you feel better in that moment. It is best to acknowledge negative thoughts when they come up and then choose not to stay with them by distracting yourself.

No one can eliminate all bad thoughts, but you can make the conscious decision to be in charge of your thinking. Filter through what is real and what needs to be focused on. Your mind is yours to control. You cannot control the first thought, but you can control the second. Choose to consciously override thoughts that weaken you. This will allow you to feel you have some personal power.

Some suggestions to explore:

- What is motivating me to obsess over this negative thought? Is it anger, guilt, or an assumption you have made? Or, something that was said or something you said?
- What can be done right now to stop focusing on this topic?
- How about walking out of the room/around the block, or finding something to do that requires focus? If you are at home you could do some chores, read something, meditate, clean, or do anything else that will allow for distraction. My personal favorite is to bring my attention to nature. Even when I am in a city, I can always look up at the sky and focus on the power of nature. There is always the old faithful of taking a few deep breaths and focusing on each inhale/exhale to break the energy of the moment. Whatever you can think of that is helpful to change your focus will give you a feeling of being a bit more grounded and less in your head.
- How will it feel to take charge and replace this thought with one that strengthens me?
- Which thoughts strengthen me?
- How can I remember to find a strengthening thought when I find myself obsessing over a negative thought? How can I remember that when a negative thought takes hold, I have the power to override it?

A most effective tool is to find an object that symbolically represents this knowledge: "I can influence what I think and therefore how I behave." The object could be anything from a rubber band or leather band around your wrist, to a drawing or photo on your phone, desk, or computer. You can put flowers or a plant on your desk – any change is good as long as it reminds you of and therefore supports you while you are breaking the habit of letting your negative thoughts rule! Whenever you see this symbolic object you are reminded of what you are working on.

If you choose to stay with a negative thought, then take responsibility for that choice! If you have a bad time as a result of this decision, you can only blame yourself. It is true that "Where there is a will, there is a way." You will be amazed how much space is created in your head once you start eliminating thoughts that weaken you. It will take some practice and, most importantly, you'll need to find the right tools that work for you. Think in terms of reprogramming your software and be patient and kind with yourself during this process.

A VERBAL ATTACK – HOW TO RESPOND

Somebody launches a verbal attack on you and you have no idea what triggered it.

It is not always so easy to recognize, let alone acknowledge that you have been verbally abused. A verbal attack is aggressive language and delivered in a manner that it feels like an attack. Sometimes it is not even the words chosen that make it an attack, but the tone alone that can be abusive. Should the person raise the volume of his or her voice, it becomes slightly more obvious that this is indeed a verbal attack. The conflict is verbal rather than physical. Sadly, people tend to mostly talk of physical attacks and ignore just how much verbal abuse there is and how damaging this truly is.

These conflicts can start in many ways including these examples:
- Children and the elderly sometimes use verbally abusive language due to the sheer frustration they are experiencing relating to their own circumstances. It still is abusive language. There is a difference between a bored teenager's attack and somebody who is letting it out on you.
- Sarcasm is seen as unexpressed anger, or anger disguised as apparent humor. This, too, can be aggressive and verbally abusive.

It is important to keep your focus on what you can influence. You are able to influence your response and your emotions around what just happened or is happening.

I keep coming back to the quote: "You cannot change people, but you can change how you react." Bearing this quote in mind, here are some helpful thoughts:
- Recognize when you are being verbally attacked.

- If possible acknowledge this is actually happening in that moment.
- Verbal attacks might not hurt your body, but you do feel them! It is not always possible to acknowledge verbal abuse when it is going on. The abusive language triggers emotions and when they are triggered it is hard to think clearly.
- If possible, step away. If not, stay quiet, and attempt to remain calm. Take a couple of breaths. The natural tendency is to respond by counterattacking, pleading, or debating, depending on the situation. Try not to do this. In the moment it serves very little purpose other than to either further aggravate the person or let him or her feel he or she has won by getting you to react.
- If you are lucky enough and can step away, give yourself time to get a clear picture of what just happened. Gaining some clarity through reflecting on the situation will help you in the future should this happen again.

To help distance yourself from people who behave in this manner or to have a better understanding of what is behind it, consider these thoughts:

- Accept that everyone has their own reality. Who knows what has happened to them in their day or life so far?
- Ask yourself, what reason, if any, there is to this attack. What is the attacker trying to accomplish? (Dump their frustration or anger, which might not even be related to you?)
- If it is not about you, accept the fact there is no need to take this behavior personally.
- Ask yourself, "If it is not about me personally, then does it need to affect me?"
- If you think this is about you, then ask yourself what reasons they might have for saying this. Is this the first time this has hap-

pened? What part of this might be justified? Do not excuse the behavior but simply attempt to see both sides.

- While the verbal abuse is going on, the ideal scenario would be to try and let it bounce off you. Easier said than done! Try your best not to react and stay silent.
- Depending on how strong you are, see if you can let them air their feelings without feeling affected.

More often than not, verbal abuse is a form of venting on the part of the attacker and has little to do with the person they are attacking.

Remember: their attack does not reflect negatively on who you are, rather on who they are.

It is good to take some time to explore your thoughts on this. Think about what you would like to achieve with your response.

Sadly, confrontation seems to be difficult to avoid these days, so be prepared to respond in a manner that allows you to stay true to yourself, and let the other person know you will not tolerate it.

ALWAYS DOING EVERYTHING YOURSELF?

Do you end up doing everything yourself? How would it be if you could ask for, or even accept the help of others?

It can be so difficult to consider asking for someone's help when you are used to coping with everything on your own. It can be uncomfortable to trust anyone to do it right, or to do it as quickly as you can do it on your own.

Today, society contains some very bizarre patterns. Consider this: You are born into a community called the family and then you grow up within communities. You have groups of friends within communities of school, work, or clubs you seek to join. As social creatures, life is set up around communities. Yet we no longer find it easy to ask for help. Whatever the reasons you do not think you can ask for help, everyone can benefit from a little support at times.

Consider this short story (author unknown):
A little boy was having difficulty lifting a heavy stone.
His father came along just then.
Noting the boy's failure, he asked, "Are you using all your strength?"
"Yes, I am," the little boy said impatiently.
"No, you are not," the father answered. "I am right here just waiting, and you haven't asked me to help you."

There is simply no need to always have to do it all alone if you are willing to change your mind-set.

If you are having trouble meeting a deadline (maybe you need to organize your schedule, complete a chore or task, or get any other job finished), and there simply is not enough time (you only have two hands), ask yourself these questions:

1. What might happen if you do not manage to finish this task?
2. On a scale of 1-10, how bad would that be?
3. Which part, if any, could be finished tomorrow instead of today?
4. Look at what part of the project is best for you to deal with yourself.
5. Which parts could you ask for help with?
6. What resources, skills, or support are available to you?
7. Once you have determined the answers to steps 1-6, consider who could provide some support to you today.
8. How do you feel about having that person's help? Is he or she the right person or are there others you could call?
9. How can you help them to help you?
10. Make a list of what steps you need to take to complete the project. Perhaps a mental list is good enough. If not, write down the list in order of priority.
11. Delegate and communicate clearly to your chosen support person(s).
12. Proceed step-by-step, knowing the task will be accomplished. It might not be today, but it will be accomplished.

As with all behavioral change, allow yourself to make this shift at a speed comfortable for you.

Self-Awareness

ON BEING JUDGMENTAL

"Everybody is judgmental; we all judge people when we see them."
This is a statement I overheard on a train once. Having grown up in
a house with two main rules – No empty threats and Everybody is
innocent until proven guilty, in other words, do not judge a book by
its cover, my immediate thought was, "Now, wait a minute" when I
heard this comment. However, as the gentleman then continued to
say, "When you see someone walking down the street who is dressed
like a thug, you think of him as a thug," I realized how, even with my
upbringing, there are times when I also label in the first instance. Underlying thoughts encourage us on some deeper level to judge.

**Not passing judgment, however, requires awareness of yourself,
your thoughts, and behavior patterns:**

- Behavior usually follows your thinking, so you will notice that
  when you give way to a negative and judgmental thought, then
  negative, disempowering behavior might follow.
- Pay some attention over the course of a day to what your
  thoughts are and what behavior they kick off.
- Give yourself twenty-four hours, ideally longer, to observe
  yourself.
- Make a note of what the situations are that trigger judgmental
  thoughts.

A judgmental person thinks and believes that who and how they
are is the correct way, hence if somebody is different, they can look
down on this person. What is right for you does not mean it is right
for someone else; in fact, it is arrogant to.think others should make
the same choices you do. Accepting someone for who he or she is
makes you a better, stronger, more loving person with your own integrity intact.

Being judgmental can come from insecurity or the need to control. There is less room for generosity and openness in such an atmosphere. I take this to be risky behavior, as you can cut off your nose to spite your face by writing someone off before you know him or her better. Judging someone can hurt both parties, as it limits where the interaction, conversation, or relationship can go. Nonjudgmental people are often openhearted, freer with their emotions, and have less need to control the environment through categorizing everything. They tend to be more at ease and comfortable within themselves and with the world around them.

Next time you catch yourself judging someone, stop and ask yourself what exactly you are feeling uncomfortable about and what you might be losing by judging someone too quickly.

Some questions to ask yourself if you wish to start moving away from the behavior pattern of being judgmental:

- What triggered this judgmental behavior in me? What just happened that made me react with judgment?
- What exactly did the person say or do, or not say or do?
- What, if anything, am I assuming about this person or this situation?
- Is my assumption stopping me from being understanding and open-hearted?
- Might there be another way to look at this?
- What might some of these other points of view be?
- What will happen if I do not manage to change my judgment of this person?
- How would that affect me?
- What is the best thing for me to do now? Think of your choices, make one, and...
- Go ahead and take that action

With increased awareness you will reach a point when you can slowly stop yourself from being judgmental.

Consider this view by Eckhart Tolle:

"If her past were your past, her pain your pain, her level of consciousness your level of consciousness, you would think and act exactly as she does. With this realization comes forgiveness, compassion, peace."

FEELING LONELY?

Feeling lonely usually starts when you believe or feel there is something missing in your life, be it intimacy, understanding, friendship, acceptance, support, a rewarding activity, or one that stimulates you and recharges your batteries. It is important to accept that loneliness is a feeling – the feeling of being alone – and not necessarily a fact. Actually, being alone and feeling lonely are not the same thing. It is possible to feel lonely whilst standing in a room full of people.

I had always thought of myself as a very outgoing, social person who thrived in the company of others. The key word being thought. I thought (consequently believed) I was a very social person. In fact, I now know that yes, I am quite social, but having time to myself is just as important to me. When I balance the two I am at my happiest. Luckily, I have learned to manage my schedule in such a way that both parts of me are happy!

When you are ready to take a closer look at your feelings of loneliness, then consider the following questions:
- What was going on before you started feeling lonely?
- What changed? What triggered the loneliness?
- What advice would you give a friend who felt lonely like you are now?
- Consider the advice you have offered. What actions have you suggested your friend take?
- How can you apply that advice to yourself?
- What would you lose by not taking your own advice?
- What would you gain from taking that advice?
- How would you feel about yourself if you managed to follow through and stop feeling lonely?

- At this point the choice is yours. Whatever advice you will have given your friend can now be applied to your situation. Maybe you chose to call a friend and ask his or her opinion as one of your own options. Other choices might include taking a walk or nap, or making plans to meet someone. Whatever proactive steps you can think of that appeal to you are amongst the choices you now have.
- Proceed with whatever decision you made.

Be pleased with yourself if you have shifted from feeling lonely to feeling better, even if it is only a little bit better. It is a step in the right direction!

The brain can rewire itself — What this means to behavioral change

Just as life is always changing, so is the brain. It is through practicing and repeating *new* behavior that you transform into the better version of yourself. Behavior can be shifted, tweaked, changed, or completely replaced with more positive empowering patterns. With practice and repetition the brain rewires itself and changes become sustainable. Science has proven this. This is fantastic news especially for anybody wishing to improve the quality of their life by making an effort to change. Making any changes in thinking patterns, or in behavior patterns, would be very difficult, if not impossible, without this scientific truth. Knowing this offers not only motivation but also confidence to continue on the path to change and transformation.

Over the last few decades, studies in neuroscience have shown the default network you were born with can be changed. This happens by creating new neural pathways. The default network ensures your survival by detecting and responding to threats, such as a tiger about to eat you! The default network generates a fight-or-flight response to increase the odds of survival. However, it can become hypersensitive, interfering with your ability to experience the present moment in a more open and relaxed manner. The production of neurochemical and molecular changes in the cells known as neurons is how the changes in the brain occur. While going through the process of learning how to think, do, or behave differently, new neurons are being produced. Neurons are messengers communicating by transmitting electrical signals.

Thoughts generate a chemical reaction in the brain. The same chemical reaction takes place every time you think the same thought – be it a negative one or a positive one. Creating new neural networks requires following through with the action step of creating new thinking and behavior patterns.

Allowing time for practice and repetition to reframe a negative thought with a positive empowering one is essential to the success of creating change. Just like exercise, the work requires repetition and activity to reinforce new learning. Thoughts and feelings have to align. In other words, you will not succeed to create new pathways by eating lots of sweets while telling yourself you are fit and healthy.

Empathy/Compassion

FORGIVENESS

Learning how to forgive allows you to close the book on certain chapters in life that otherwise stay with you like a heavy suitcase you have to carry everywhere. Forgiveness is important to learn. If you do not forgive and forget along the way, imagine just how much baggage you will be carrying with you. Luckily, our minds do have a tendency to forget some things. Normally these are the things that do not carry any emotional attachment. However, in situations where you are hurt, your habitual patterns of response are triggered. When you feel you are the object of disrespect or abuse, your mind does not forget so quickly. I imagine pain sits in the heart, which is your emotional body, not in the mind; hence it is harder to just forget. In order to forget and forgive, some healing is required. Forgiveness and healing are closely linked.

The act of forgiveness is a process involving you, not the other person. If the result of a situation makes you blame the other person for the outcome, along with your blame, you are giving them responsibility for your feelings and well-being.

Accepting that you are willing to forgive, and learning how to forgive, are part of taking responsibility for the quality of your life. Forgiving someone does not mean that you accept or overlook their behavior, but means you wish to move forward from the pain you felt. You do not want to carry this particular suitcase full of pain with you as permanent baggage. You choose to make some space for something new, something more positive to come into your life.

Forgiving someone can bring up fears of loss. If you forgive them, you might have to let them go mainly because you no longer wish to have their type of behavior in your life. You have chosen a life of personal growth and development. They have not. Everybody has the right to make their own choices and live life aligned with their wishes and goal. This can mean the best choice is to go separate ways. No matter how difficult this thought could be, it also could be the best thing you can do for them. Forgive them and thereby set each other free.

8

EMOTIONAL INTELLIGENCE AT WORK

E motional intelligence is an important factor at work, affecting almost everything you do. The skills that come with an increased level of emotional intelligence are also known as soft skills. They apply both to the understanding of yourself and of others. If someone has emotional intelligence, he or she is attuned to his or her own feelings and can empathize with others on the basis of this. Understanding your own feelings enables you to recognize and interpret emotions in others, seeing how these emotions enter into their behavior and attitudes. This also means that you can act on your perceptions in a productive manner.

I concentrate here on a particular application: at work. Companies have become increasingly more aware of the need to include coaching and training of these soft skills. Understanding emotional intelligence is central for change management, which is based on the emotional intelligence skills of the whole workforce.

Emotional intelligence can be developed through learning the appropriate life skills (time and stress management, empathy, compassion, interpersonal skills, prioritizing) and applying them at work. I offer a small selection of exercises to help.

INCREASE YOUR EMOTIONAL INTELLIGENCE TO BE MORE EFFECTIVE AT WORK

More and more, the world of coaching witnesses how frequently a lack of emotional intelligence (EQ) defines the difference between a merely good businessperson and a successful one. What we mean by successful in this case is a person who is confident, strong, empathic, effective, productive, inspiring, and efficient at managing time and stress levels. Such a person will feel and be truly comfortable at work.

Today the concept of EQ is having a strong impact on the business and corporate world. It is now accepted that a well-developed EQ allows a manager or team member to restrain less productive feelings and focus on his or her goals with more positive feelings. Such a person will be a self-confident, open communicator who inspires other people; anger, self-doubt, and stress will not be in evidence.

Emotional intelligence is defined as having the ability to recognize and understand emotions and their impact on behavior and attitudes, especially in others. Those who have a high degree of emotional intelligence are able to understand their own feelings and thus tune into how others are feeling, with the result that they can act on their perceptions in a truly productive manner.

Having emotional intelligence includes possessing a level of awareness in the areas of: self-management, self-esteem, motivational skills, empathy, interaction skills, self-confidence, relationship management, stress management, time management, and emotional self-awareness.

An individual's EQ affects almost everything he or she does. For example, if you work in a solitary setting, the quality of your work is determined by your self-esteem and self-confidence. Both help in keeping you motivated and inspired.

For those in the corporate world in search of leadership and change, various studies show that CEOs make many of their decisions intuitively, mainly because in this fast-moving world there is not enough time to wait for all the facts. Thus a leader's best thinking and decision-making is grounded as much in their EQ as their IQ. There is significant evidence that the skills a person with a high EQ brings to bear have a significant impact on organizational performance.

The good news is that whilst the IQ is relatively fixed, EQ can be developed. For this reason, more and more companies are hiring psychologists and life coaches to improve the standard of their management by increasing the EQ of their managers. An organization that fails to recognize the need for emotional intelligence in its culture does so at its peril.

RELEASE THAT HAPPY HORMONE FOR MOTIVATION

Dopamine, one of the four key neurotransmitters, acts as a chemical messenger helping transmission of signals in the brain. When something good happens, a chain reaction goes off in your brain. Your reward system is activated which increases not only your attention, but also positive feedback. One of the results is motivation.

To stay motivated you can keep the stream of dopamine flowing with positive actions, such as the following:

- Physical exercise – before, during your lunch break, or after work.
- You can take a walk around the block which will get some energy flowing during the course of the working day. A ten-minute walk is better than nothing at all. You will feel good about yourself for at least having taken the ten minutes.
- Meditation – this could come in the form of taking some time out to sit and do nothing, just sit or walk around the block alone.
- Healthy living habits – good nutrition, enough sleep, and downtime. If you cannot get enough sleep or downtime on a regular basis aim for once per week or every other weekend.
- Treating yourself kindly by acknowledging successes. No matter how small this success might be, acknowledge it. Your brain will like the positive feedback you are giving it by acknowledging a success and will release some of the happy hormone.

Dopamine is a powerful chemical that decreases your stress reaction. Stress depletes the levels of dopamine, which can lead to a dopamine deficiency.

Dopamine deficiency can result in:

- Loss of energy and joie de vivre
- Lack of focus
- Difficulty concentrating
- Feeling down
- Lack of motivation and drive
- Mood swings
- Inability to reach goals

Managers and leaders who believe in motivating using fear will, in fact, get the opposite effect. Fear results in stress, and stress will demotivate. When the survival mode kicks in based on perceived fear, the emotions involved are disruptive to cognitive resources. All in all, not a good situation!

On the other hand, the release of dopamine and the feeling of motivation that results are of utmost value. Leaders would do well to bear this in mind when they are not able to motivate by ruling with fear-based tactics.

With techniques in place helping you manage long working hours, lack of sleep, and other inhibitors of the work environment, you will automatically be releasing some of this happy hormone. Learning the soft skills that support balancing the ups and downs of life means you are adding strengths.

ASKING FOR SUPPORT AT WORK

It can be so difficult to even consider asking for someone's help when you are used to handling everything on your own. Whatever the reasons behind this, we can all benefit from a little support sometimes. How would it be if you could ask for help and trust others enough to accept their help in getting the job done?

Suggestions for team leaders:

As a team leader or manager, knowing how to ask for help and being comfortable accepting it is a vital part of your success. As the person in charge, your ability to select, delegate, motivate, facilitate growth, and align your team is one of the top priorities. With this you will be establishing a focused, solid, and cooperative team that will be easier to lead. Your responsibility is making sure the right people not only come together, but also work together productively.

Asking for help includes knowing when to say no to being involved in a problem that is not yours alone to solve. If you have delegated properly and are confident your team has all the support necessary, you have taken care of your side of the job. If you allow the person who is responsible to cover this issue, you are saying no to your belief that you have to handle everything on your own. With this, you are saying yes to allow someone to help you... leaders are to encourage people to make independent decisions as it greatly improves motivation. Fostering this involves asking for their help. The necessary time to think about the team's goals and performance will be created by accepting this help.

As a coworker in a team you are also in a position that requires asking for help at times. You might not be able to completely understand part of a project or the vision expressed in it, so asking a colleague to brainstorm with you would help. You hesitate to ask, however, because you make the assumption they will think less of you or your abilities. Good team players share information, knowledge, and experience, and are comfortable asking for help. If you are open to a request for assistance and take the initiative to offer help, then asking for it yourself falls under being a good team player and coworker.

Ask yourself these questions if you wish to find a way to feel more comfortable with asking for help:

1. What might happen if I do not ask for help or support?
2. On a scale of 1-10, how bad would that be?
3. What will happen if I do not get this completed, sorted out, or clarified?
4. What will happen if I do complete, sort out, or get clarification?
5. Imagine the two scenarios and consider what your next step will be at this point.
6. Who can you ask for help? What resources and skills do you already have to support this situation?
7. How do you feel about having that person's help? Is he or she the right person, or are there others you could call upon?
8. How can you help them to help you? What exactly do you need to communicate to them in order for them to help you in the way you need it?
9. Make a list of steps you need to take to complete the project. Maybe a mental list is good enough. If not, write down the list in order of priority.
10. Delegate and communicate clearly to your chosen support person(s).
11. Realize that next time it will already be easier to ask, since you now have some practice!

Enjoy the extra time you will have and the feeling of strength that comes with feeling the team spirit.

MONDAY MORNING BLUES

There are many reasons for having the Monday morning blues. As an entrepreneur or self-employed it is also possible not to feel enthusiastic about Monday morning. The Monday morning blues do not necessarily relate only to disliking the job/company, a stressful work environment, or difficult interpersonal relationships at work. Sometimes you might simply be working too much, the hours are too long, or you have not made the most of the weekends for recharging your battery.

Here are some thoughts to help when the blues set in:

If the blues already start on Sunday evening, ask yourself the following questions:

- What exactly is going on that makes you feel like this now? Perhaps you did not finish something on Friday that you should have. Or perhaps there is somebody in the office you are dreading to see because you have an unresolved issue. Perhaps you are not feeling well because you do not take good enough care of yourself (eating poorly, not getting enough exercise, enough sleep, enough downtime, or enough playtime).

Realize what a shame it would be to ruin Sunday evening.
Think about what you can do to feel a bit more positive.

It helps to plan ahead:

1. If your attention is required to resolve an upcoming Monday morning problem at work, then take some time to think about what you need to do. Do you have to prepare something, organize your thoughts about a necessary conversation, plan shopping for food, or fit a walk into your schedule?

2. Once you organize your thoughts, if you still dislike the thought of going to work, then perhaps it is the job itself that is causing your blues. A change might be in order – perhaps a change of perspective about work.

Some thoughts on how to change your perspective:
- Most things cannot be changed overnight. Yet since you will be going to work the next day, take a moment to consider what your job does do for your life; for example, paying the rent, putting food onto the table, clothes onto your back.
- Bring the focus on to the positive to put your thoughts into perspective. Consider what is good about your job. What other aspects – besides your paycheck – are positive? For example, do you like the team you work with or the tasks you do? Have you learned a lot? Do you enjoy the environment, company, location, colleagues where you work? Do you enjoy the challenges it brings as compared to a less challenging job?

Make Monday morning as pleasant as possible:
Personally I find this step most helpful in the times when I am feeling a bit tired or have been traveling for work too much.
- If possible, organize something on Sunday to shorten your morning preparation time. For example, decide what you will wear to work, pack your snack or lunch, and choose an activity that you would otherwise do in the morning that you can take care of on Sunday. This will help decrease some of the hectic morning rush.
- Practice acceptance. You will be going to work in the morning and no amount of moaning about it will change that fact. If anything, moaning will simply ruin your Sunday evening. Is this the choice you want to make?
- Take Monday off if possible, or schedule a home office day.

- Let nature offer some of its energy: On your way to work, draw some inspiration from nature, which contains so much energy and has so much to offer. Make sure to "stop and smell the roses" – if only by looking out of the window. It is possible to find nature everywhere.

Finding a new, improved frame of mind helps you get rid of the Monday morning blues. The choice is yours.

MANAGE YOUR STRESS

In all aspects of one's life, especially in the business world, heightened emotional intelligence (EQ) strengthens and augments the following social skills:

- Successfully and proactively coping with life's demands and pressures. (Stress management)
- Building rewarding relationships with others. (Social skills)
- Seeking first to understand, then to be understood. Required here are, for example, empathy, respect, and listening skills.
- The self-confidence to act with authority and to handle tough decisions.
- Leading by example.
- Inspiring by example.
- Getting the most out of others with respect.
- Establishing direction with a sense of clarity and understanding.
- Motivating with encouragement and support.
- Energizing with ease.
- Not dropping the ball.
- Holding the big picture clearly enough to connect the dots.
- Seeing that the glass is always half full – being a positive thinker.
- Managing time effectively. (Time management)

From this, it can be seen that having a high EQ is extremely important. One of the skills that is most necessary is the ability to manage stress in the moment. Try the following if you find yourself in a position when it is all too much.

Stress Management Techniques:
- If possible, take a break and leave the room. Find a quiet space, even the bathroom will do. Compose yourself by focusing on

taking at least three breaths. As you exhale, imagine a little bit of the tension leaving your body. (I find it helpful to visualize a dark cloud dissipating.)

- If it is not possible, make a mental note to address the issue later when you have time and can focus on this.
- Gather your thoughts.
- Keep your focus on exactly what has been going on that is causing you the stress. Is it the task itself? How about something more basic such as hunger or the space around you? Does it involve another person or people? What is missing?
- Once you know specifically what has thrown you off balance, think about what you can now do to influence the situation.
- Consider all the steps required to find a solution. Make a list, if only a mental one. What can you do today, right now?
- Order your list in terms of priority. What has to be done first, then what?
- Consider the practicalities of your action plan. Is it realistic? Have you the time? Do you need advice or support? If so, whose?
- Fine-tune the steps you consider necessary to resolve the situation. Keep things realistic to avoid feeling pressure.
- Having thought things through you may find your perspective on the problem has changed. Adjust the plan accordingly.
- It is most important to ensure that any action you propose to take is in keeping with your personality and can be executed in a style that suits you.
- Remind yourself that life is constantly changing and the only thing you can control is your reaction to events – not the events themselves!

Be aware that improving your emotional intelligence is a constant work in progress.

UNWINDING AFTER WORK

How about going out for a sail, swim, drink, run, or meet friends, play with your children, talk to your partner – without your head still being full of work-related information? It can be difficult to leave work-related thoughts behind at the end of the day. Too many people arrive home and are not really present. Their body might have walked through the door but mentally they are miles away.

This is a common topic with my coaching clients. I might work with five different clients all on this particular topic, yet each one will find his or her own unique way to help themselves unwind and reenter their personal life.

First of all, it helps to remember and accept as an important truth that your work is only *part* of your life. It is wonderful if you love what you do and have passion for your work, but do not forget that your personal life is at least as important as your work.

The goal is not to neglect your work but also *not* neglect your family, friends, and self. Establish and maintain a routine of self-care – start by unwinding from work on your way home. Some examples that help my clients include: listening to music or an audiobook in the car or on the train, taking a walk and being more mindful while doing so, meeting a friend, or exercise. Start instilling this habit and you will experience life as more satisfying, rewarding, happy, and healthier in mind and body.

Periods of downtime are necessary in order to avoid burning out. The less stress all around, the better your performance will be. This is more than true of work.

Some helpful suggestions to consider for de-stressing and leaving work at the office:

- Accept that only on a rare occasion will you be able to go home leaving a clear desk behind. There is always more to do!
- Raise your awareness to how many I shoulds you have running!

- Attempt to let go of at least one I should thought. They guarantee that you will be taking the stress with you. If you are used to I should thoughts, they might be a bad habit at this point. Know that letting go of old habits requires time and patience. I should thoughts could also be based on a limiting belief (a thought pattern that limits you, holds you back, and can keep you running in circles. These are best explored with a professional coach if you are finding it difficult to shift).

- To start, focus on making one small change – one baby step at a time will lead to sustainable transformation.

- For motivation: Ask yourself how de-stressing and leaving work at the office will benefit you. Write down what you will gain. Writing it down makes the desire to change more real.

- Take some time to consider what the best, most practical and realistic steps are for you to take. For example: What would you have to do to treat your commute home as a time to unwind? (Stop for a coffee, take a stroll in the park or around the block, sit and watch the stressed people on their way home and be thankful that you are not going to be one of them anymore.)

Be realistic with your thoughts and plans for this change. Find whatever best matches your personality, fits into your lifestyle, suits you the best, and would give you the best rewards. For some it might be a visualization of putting work into a box and leaving it in a drawer at the office.

Allow yourself as much time as you need to find what routine works best for you. You, your family, and friends will be grateful.

If you have had a particularly bad day, make sure you allow a little extra time for unwinding and de-stressing.

Remind yourself that work will still be there in the morning. With a fresh approach, a de-stressed self, a good night's sleep, a good dinner, a laugh, etc., you will be able to tackle all issues with better energy and a better attitude.

Leaving work behind, mentally and physically, is up to you.

In summary: If you want to do this, have found the right motivation, then consider your choices and follow through. It will take time and practice until this new behavior is in place. The rewards will be worth the effort. Your boss will appreciate the stronger you and so will your friends and family. Remember, you get the most out of this as you are treating yourself with the care and respect you deserve.

Saying no to something makes room for a yes to something else. In this case, no to stress and work at the end of the day means yes to yourself and the personal part of your life.

If one approach you decided to try out does not seem to be working too well, try another one!

9

SOME FINAL THOUGHTS: WHAT WORKS FOR ME

A happy, successful, enriched life requires know-how – a series of life skills that help you manage your personal and working life with greater ease and confidence.

Here are the life skills that work for me:

- Knowing that I have the tools to deal with problems when they arise.
- Knowing I always have a choice... if only to walk out of the room for a moment to gather myself.
- Knowing how to break any problem down into small, more manageable steps.
- Knowing how to see a problem with different eyes in order to find a solution.
- Knowing how to find the strength to deal with an issue, obstacle, or dilemma when I feel a lack of energy.
- Knowing who to go to for support, if only for a hug in that moment.
- Knowing what exercise to use if I feel anger, fear, guilt, or any other strong emotion.

154 · SUZIE DOSCHER

- Knowing how to say no when necessary and appropriate.
- Knowing that saying no means I am saying yes to something else!
- And finally, the knowledge that I can cope with anything because I have the necessary life skills.

I know what is possible if you really put your heart, soul, and mind into it – that is what I tell my clients and is based on my own life.

10

The BALANCE
Workbook

WHAT YOU WILL GAIN FROM COMPLETING THIS WORKBOOK SECTION:

- *Awareness* – becoming aware of something is the first and most important step in the process of change. It can often be the most difficult one. The good news is that with awareness you have already "reframed" how you see a situation or an issue.
- *Clarity* – giving yourself a reality check by working through this book and answering the questions helps you gain a broader perspective of how things really are. Working out what has to change will lead to bringing more balance into your life.
- *A sense of direction* – – exploring the key aspects of your present and past gives you a better sense of where you want to be heading in the future – a different perspective of your old and new dreams and goals.
- *Action* – by working this book you are already taking action..
- *Wisdom* – you will come to realize that success requires time, patience, practice, and repetition, as well as making mistakes, to succeed. This wisdom increases your Emotional Intelligence, which is "the successful or unsuccessful management of your emotions. Managing them plays a critical role in the overall success and happiness of your life." In the world of business, "CEOs are hired for their intellect and business expertise – and fired for a lack of emotional intelligence."

HOW TO USE THIS WORKBOOK:

- Use a notebook or journal that you will dedicate to your Balance project. Write down the questions at the top of each page, so you have plenty of room for answers and you can refer back to your questions and answers easily.

- The Workbook can be the first, active step on your path of personal growth and development, or as a periodic reality check. The questions are designed to help you examine and explore where you want to be in the future and where you are in your life right now. In a sense, you will be brainstorming with yourself.

- Work through each section ignoring any questions that are not relevant to you or returning to them at a later date. There is no "I have to do this right now." Each person perceives the situation from their view, each has their own unique experiences, background, and reality, so do not think there are right or wrong answers.

- If you are not sure what to write, just start writing. You will be amazed what might come to the surface.

- Work through it step-by-step, focus on the chapter most relevant to your life right now, or skip around depending on what information, clarity, or outcome you are looking fo.

- If writing your answers alone does not appeal to you, feel free to use pictures, drawings, mind mapping, or whatever suits your style and personality. Allow yourself to be as free and creative as you like.

With the information gained from the Workbook, refer back to the areas of the Handbook for relevant topics to further your growth and development.

THE OVERALL ASSESSMENT YOU ARE GETTING FROM THIS WORKBOOK SECTION IS DIVIDED INTO THREE SECTIONS:

Your Future — Your Dreams, Goals, and Aspirations

Your Present — A Reality Check

Your Past — Leave It In the Past

1. YOUR FUTURE-
Your Dreams, Goals and Aspirations

E xplore where you want to go, how you want it to look, and who you want to be going into your future.

Overview

WE ARE GOING TO COVER THE FOLLOWING AREAS:
- Overall assessment of goals and dreams
- Your comfort zone
- Letting go of any regrets
- Designing the future
- Making it happen

PART 1: EXPLORATION AND FACT GATHERING

1. Which dreams and/or goals have you already achieved?

2. What goals are you keen on achieving in the near- or long-term future?

3. Do you regret any unfulfilled dreams? If yes, should any be re-considered?

4. Define your comfort zone. What are you comfortable doing? What comes easily and naturally?

5. What is outside your comfort zone? What do you think and feel would be uncomfortable if you had to do it differently? What approach have you never dared to try? What do you shy away from but would love to do?

6. List your goals and dreams in a realistic and prioritized order.

What jumped out at you from this exploration?

- Choose to explore one goal at a time – which one will you pursue now?

Big goals usually have to be broken down into a series of smaller goals. Remember, it is one step at a time that gets you to the top of the ladder.

PART 2: ACTION PLAN

1. Make peace with any regrets you have. Accept that sometimes things do not happen for a reason. If you find this difficult, consult a professional or talk it over with a trusted friend.

2. With reference to the goal you have chosen to pursue now, ask yourself: What would be the ideal outcome?

3. What compromises are you willing to make in order to achieve this goal?

4. Which compromises are you not willing to make?

5. Who are you doing this for, if not yourself?

6. Whose support do you wish to have and/or need?

7. What specific actions come next? Do you have to research some-thing, consult someone, learn a new skill, or tweak any existing skills?

8. Prioritize the next steps. If you are feeling overwhelmed, please bear in mind that one step at a time will get you up the ladder. Sometimes the steps are smaller than you wish them to be. How-ever, feeling success from taking steps, no matter which size, will keep you motivated.

9. Give yourself positive feedback or reward yourself in some way.

Keep track of your progress, updating your action plan as necessary. When the time is right, follow this exercise for the next goal you have on your list.

IF NECESSARY:
Who might support you/hold you accountable/give you feedback?

WHAT NOT TO FORGET:

AFFIRMATION:
Based on your exploration, summarize your thoughts and feelings with a positive statement – an affirmation. Affirmations have the abil-ity to help with the process of rewiring your brain. They are a proven method for self-improvement. With practice and repetition the brain can rewire itself. A positive statement releases feel-good hormones rather than the stress hormones released by negative thoughts. Using affirmations supports breaking negative thought patterns.

Louise Hay, one of the founders of the self-help movement, states; "An affirmation opens the door. It is a beginning point on the path to change. In essence, you are saying to your subconscious mind: "I am taking responsibility. I am aware that there is something I can do to change."

TO SUMMARIZE THIS SECTION, SELECT ONE OR CREATE YOUR OWN AFFIRMATION, USING THE 3 P'S:
- Positive
- Present
- Personal

The statement should be positive, be written in the present tense, and be personal to you.

Please make this personal, use your own words, and make sure it rings true for you.

SOME EXAMPLES TO SPARK IDEAS:

I am living the life I want

or

I am working toward a more balanced life

or

I make the right choices for me

or

_____

Post your personal statement wherever you can see it on a regular basis and read it frequently.

2. YOUR PRESENT

This is the "reality check" section. By this I mean taking stock and gaining an overview of your life as it is, looking at what is working and what is not. Remember, sometimes life is going to be "as good as you are handling it" on a daily basis.

Some areas might be more difficult to cope with, handle, or keep balanced. Others can be enhanced, tweaked, or even changed completely, but there will always be areas where "this is as good as it gets" for the time being.

Handling those moments is the key to feeling balanced. Being aware of your expectations and managing them – keeping them real – is vital for your success.

Overview

WE ARE GOING TO COVER THE FOLLOWING AREAS:
- How your life is in the present
- What is important to you
- What is of value to you in your life
- What is working
- What is not working
- What has to happen to ensure a more balanced life

PART 1: EXPLORATION AND FACT GATHERING
Picture your life as you live it now. What is it like? How does it feel? Describe it:

1. Picture your life as you live it now. What is it like? How does it feel? Describe it:

2. Explore your relationships. Describe how you fare as a:
   a. Partner
   b. Parent
   c. Sibling
   d. Neighbor
   e. Friend
   f. Member of your community

3. Examine these six facets of your life. How satisfied are you in these areas:
   a. Home
   b. Career
   c. Health
   d. Financial Health
   e. Fun
   f. Personal Growth

4. What brings value to your life?

5. What distracts you from being on track?

6. What drains you?

7. What motivates you?

8. List all that is working and need not change.

9. List whatever you are not willing to give up or change.

10. List all that is not working and could use improving or eliminating.

11. Which routines, if any, could use refreshing, altering, modifying, or replacing?

12. What is the first change you want to make?

PART 2: ACTION PLAN

If you have discovered there is more than one area that needs improving, work through one area at a time using the approach outlined below. It is of the utmost importance that you design a plan that is realistic. Any changes will take time, repetition, and patience, so do not waste your time and disappoint yourself with expectations that cannot be met. One small step at a time will get you there. When it comes to change "walk, do not run" is the healthiest approach.

Do not hesitate to ask for help if you need it. Sometimes brainstorming with a friend or professional makes the world of difference. Talking and hearing yourself think is incredibly helpful.

1. When you look at how you described each area of your life, which do you now feel deserves some attention?

2. Taking into consideration "what jumped out at you from this exploration" and your list of "what is not working," what do you want to focus on first? Consider which aspect would make the biggest difference in your life right now and is therefore your priority.

3. Examine your list of what is not working and put it in order of priority.

4. Now create your action plan. For example, if you want to make some changes in your home, start considering what is realistic, how and when you can create the time to follow through. Or, if your focus relates to your health or relationships, determine the next steps to take. What specific changes will bring you more balance?

Keep your plan SMART (Specific, Measurable, Action-Oriented, Realistic, and Time Framed).

IF NECESSARY:
Who might support you/hold you accountable /give you feedback?

WHAT NOT TO FORGET:

AFFIRMATION:
Based on your exploration, summarize your thoughts and feelings with a positive statement – an affirmation.

REMEMBER TO CREATE THIS STATEMENT APPLYING THE 3 P'S:
- Positive
- Present
- Personal

Please make this personal, use your own words, and make sure it rings true for you.

Post your personal statement wherever you can see it on a regular basis and read it frequently.

SAMPLES TO SPARK IDEAS:
Living in the "now" gives me energy

or

My life is balanced

or

I am handling my life well

or

I value the opportunities to learn new lessons

or

_____

3. YOUR PAST

Everybody has a past.
Living in the past, however, robs you of the present, the present moment, the "now."

Living in the past, however, robs you of the present, the present moment, the "now."

In my coaching practice, exploring some of the "baggage" filled with issues relating to your past is necessary to find out what exactly you are still hanging on to. Pain that remains should be healed, and beliefs that sabotage you with constricting behavior patterns should be replaced by healthier patterns.

Enjoy your happy, loving, and exciting memories. Allow them to energize you, offering you creativity and inspiration, but do not hang on to anything no longer of value. Explore it, examine it, heal it, and move on.

Letting go of the past and living in the present while looking toward the future is rejuvenating.

OVERVIEW:
Start by exploring where you stand in relation to your past and how it might be affecting your present-day life. You might still be holding on to old thinking patterns that are no longer relevant.

These will have created behavior patterns, which are limiting and disempowering for how you wish to live your life.

WE ARE GOING TO COVER THE FOLLOWING AREAS:
- Acknowledging the good and bad from the past
- Exploring what you are thankful for

- Considering what had to happen for you to be where you are now
- What and/or whom (including yourself) to stop judging
- Any unfinished business and/or open ends

PART 1: EXPLORATION AND FACT GATHERING

1. What was good about your past? What are you thankful for?

2. What still has a negative and/or disempowering hold on you? Such as thoughts, feelings, people, and so on.

3. What old habits still control some of your behavior?

4. List successes in the past.

5. What had to happen for you to have that success?

6. Whom (including yourself) are you still judging and/or blaming relating to the past?

7. Whom can you thank, and what for?

8. What do you have to accept? This could be accepting someone's limitations and therefore reducing your expectations or making them more realistic. I like the quote: "You cannot change people, but you can change how you react to them."

9. Who do you need to talk to, ask something of, or gain a better understanding of?

10. Are there any open ends or unresolved issues? (Such as physical, financial, environmental)

WHAT JUMPED OUT AT YOU FROM THIS EXPLORATION?

WHAT NOT TO FORGET I.E.:

Today I am _____thanks to

_____

or

_____

AFFIRMATION:

If you feel a positive statement in the form of an affirmation would be a helpful way to summarize your past as you move on from it, then do not forget to make it positive and in the present tense.

SOME SAMPLES:

My past is now history

or

I do not let my past affect my present

or

I am grateful for the lessons from my past

or

Without my past I would not be me

or

_____

Help yourself stay on track and reach those goals so that you can make your dreams come true.

Refer to "Letting go of the past" (page 17) to offer you some support with moving forward.

Living a more peaceful and calm life was always one of my goals – I have achieved exactly that by using this approach.

I wish you the same.

FURTHER REFERENCES

Jeffers, Ph.D., Susan. *Feel the Fear... and Do It Anyway.* Random House (UK and Ebury Press, 1987 – 2012).

Tolle, Eckhart. *The Power of Now* (Novato, CA: New World Editions, 2004).

"Victim Recovery" quoted from *Courage to Change* (Al Anon Family Group Headquarters, 1992).

Personal Bill of Rights: an excerpt from "Healing the Child Within" (1987) by Charles L. Whitfield, M.D.

Suzie Doscher

An experienced and successful professional Life and Executive coach, her practical, common sense and encouraging approach to personal development draw an international client base to Suzie. Born in New York, educated in Switzerland and England, she now resides permanently in Switzerland.

With her international upbringing, Suzie is comfortable with cross-cultural lifestyles. Continuous education and self-reflection spur on her own personal development. A strong believer in "keep on moving forward," she sees opportunities to learn in everyday occurrences.

Suzie always knew her heart was at its happiest when helping people. Her vision that everyone has access to techniques supporting personal growth and development is how this book was born.

www.suziedoscher.com

ACKNOWLEDGMENTS

Thank you to Kevin Anderson & Associates, New York.

Special thanks to my editor Stephanie Elliot for her hard work.

20925220R00108

Made in the USA
Middletown, DE
11 December 2018